THE SEARCH FOR A METHOD

IN AMERICAN STUDIES

The Search for a Method in American Studies

by

Cecil F. Tate

UNIVERSITY OF MINNESOTA PRESS
Minneapolis

Library of Congress Catalog Card Number: 73-77714

ISBN 0-8166-0700-1

Figure 3 on page 143 is taken from *Claude Lévi-Strauss* by
Edmund Leach. Copyright © 1970 by Edmund Leach.
Reprinted by permission of The Viking Press, Inc. Figure
4 on page 143 is taken from *The Structure of Art* by Jack
Burnham; reprinted with the permission of the publisher.
Copyright © 1971 by George Braziller, Inc. Quotations
from the following are used by permission of the publishers:
The American Adam by R. W. B. Lewis (University of Chicago
Press); *The Continuity of American Poetry* by Roy Harvey
Pearce (Princeton University Press); *Virgin Land* by Henry Nash Smith
(Harvard University Press); *Andrew Jackson, Symbol for an Age* by
John William Ward (Oxford University Press).

FOR MY MOTHER AND FATHER

Acknowledgments

Intellectual debts are never fully repaid and I know well the extent of my obligations to teachers and writers who are not mentioned here.

However, my indebtedness to a few people has been very great. I must thank Albert Stone, Jr., and Peter Dowell of Emory University for reading parts of this book several times and for their valuable comments on methodology in American Studies. I am particularly indebted to Robert H. L. Wheeler of Emory University for his aid and advice and for encouraging me to continue writing the book when I would gladly have put it aside.

Harold Kolb, Jr., of the University of Virginia and John Hague of Stetson University gave suggestions which I found helpful in rewriting the manuscript. Professor Kolb, especially, contributed numerous insights and criticisms which forced me to reconsider parts of my work.

I want to thank Paul Doherty, my colleague at Boston College, for his stimulating discussion of Noam Chomsky and for pointing the way for me to the discoveries of structuralist writers in several fields. The staff of the University of Minnesota Press contributed helpfully of their skills during the publication process. Norman Abrams of Boston drew the figures.

An author usually saves his final thanks for his wife and I am no different in that respect. But seldom does an author freely admit, as I do, that his wife's name really belongs on the title page as co-author. So lastly, I want to thank Sandy, whose presence is here on every page.

C. F. T.

Chestnut Hill, Massachusetts
March 1973

Table of Contents

THE SEARCH FOR A METHOD

IN AMERICAN STUDIES

Prologue: American Studies and the Problem of Method

When I began this book, method was to me already more than merely a conceptual problem. I was convinced that method, especially in the humanities, has a much deeper significance than is often thought. At the outset I was puzzled by what certain writers on American culture were saying, puzzled by not only their statements but their assumptions and the implications of what they said. I wondered if there was something that could be validly called method in American Studies. But there was a larger issue that concerned me: the meaning of method in human affairs. Of all American writers, Thoreau, perhaps, has been most aware that method is an extension of man, that the way a man approaches a problem defines the man, whether it is a problem of economy or planting beans or raising a chimney or making a book.

Thus the quarrels among academicians about method, which at first glance must seem to many of our students dry academic cavils, can be and often are highly significant because the way in which we approach a subject has a profound effect on our entire posture toward life. Thoreau, like all modern poets, was sensible of living at a perilous moment in history. Scholars must be one with poets in being sensible of both new and old dangers. Peril may be involved even in the method we use to deal with our problems as scholars.

The peril I dimly saw in the work of some writers on American culture was the danger of a further fragmentation of man in an already

3

fragmented world. Paradoxically these same writers seemed to be engaged in a response to what they conceived as the atomization of human experience. The danger, I thought, lay in unstated and unexamined methodological assumptions upon which research rested.

The question of methodology in American Studies has been debated by scholars for many years. In 1961, citing Emerson's authority, Leo Marx called for the kind of American scholar who could synthesize knowledge of his national past, the kind of man Emerson called the "delegated intellect" of his community, more interested in ideas than the majority of professional academic men — in other words, an intellectual fully engaged politically and philosophically aware. He would have to be a man able and willing to "range widely among general ideas — in philosophy, history, and literary criticism."[1] Only such a man could give us a total vision of reality, a feel for the whole of living, a basis for being a whole man. Only such a man could overcome the current trend in American scholarship toward overspecialized, minute studies of portions of the whole. Only he could make use of the enormous mass of "objective" and "empirical" data compiled by the specialists. Only he could put the pieces together, could give us a sense of totality, "the real fountain of a culture's power." The findings of the social sciences must be used, Marx concludes, but must be transcended so that American Studies scholars can develop a method of their own which moves toward a vision of the whole. At the time very few men capable of developing such a method were on the scene: Richard Chase, Richard Hofstadter, Perry Miller, David Potter, Henry Nash Smith, and C. Vann Woodward.[2]

Six years later (May 1967) Professor Marx responded to an invitation to speak to a group of historians about the methods of American Studies.[3] In his address Marx has not changed his mind about the need for humanists who can synthesize knowledge, and yet he seems to have developed serious reservations about the possibility of outlining a consistent set of methodological premises and procedures. He asks, "In what sense can American Studies be said to have a method?" and replies that perhaps the definitive answer has been given by Henry Nash Smith. In "Can 'American Studies' Develop a Method?" Smith suggested that nothing even close to a codifiable over-all method was foreseeable. Although "thirteen years have passed," comments Marx, "there is no reason to think that today Smith would need to change that assertion in any significant way."[4] Marx goes even further. If by method or procedures we mean a method and procedures borrowed, however indirectly, from the physical sciences, then, he concludes, it is neither desirable nor possible for American Studies to develop a method. No matter how the American Studies scholar has approached his subject, he has placed the key phrase *as a whole* at the center of the processes of analysis.[5]

I, for one, agree with Professor Marx that the phrase *as a whole* is the key to the approach American Studies scholars have been taking to their work in the last few years. No doubt it is neither desirable nor possible for American Studies to derive its own method, however circuitously, from the methods of the physical sciences. Yet I remain more deeply persuaded than Professor Marx that the best work in American Studies shares certain basic assumptions and *systematic* procedures.[6] I believe these assumptions and procedures can be outlined.

Equally, I am convinced that the proliferation of *theories* about American culture, however fruitful and suggestive they are, are not nearly so fruitful or so richly suggestive as the scholarly work that has actually been accomplished. What is needed then is an elucidation of those assumptions and procedures by an investigation and analysis of some of the best work in the field. If certain of those assumptions and procedures prove untenable (as I fear), then they can be rejected or reworked by scholars concerned with the theoretical foundations of the study of American culture.

Accordingly, in this book I will examine four works: *The Continuity of American Poetry* by Roy Harvey Pearce, *Virgin Land* by Henry Nash Smith, *Andrew Jackson, Symbol for an Age* by John William Ward, and *The American Adam* by R. W. B. Lewis. Each of these works is by a distinguished scholar; three are well-known literary critics as well. These men are eclectic, in the best sense of that word, and attempt to combine some of the methods and insights of American criticism of the 1930s, 1940s, and 1950s both with the results of studies stimulated by nineteenth-century Orientalists and students of myth and with some of the assumptions and techniques of contemporary social science. The rich synthesis reflected in the published products of these and other contemporary cultural critics is a recent development and marks a new direction for literary scholarship in this country, a direction which is opposed to New Criticism, the dominant mode of literary scholarship in the recent past.

With its emphasis on literature as literature, the *effect* of New Criticism in America was the isolation of the literary work of art from its human origin and cultural setting. This produced a decline in sociohistorical studies of literature which many scholars came to believe were hopelessly superficial. However, in the almost three decades since the end of World War II there has developed heightened interest in understanding American "culture" in some kind of total or comprehensive view. This mood has affected many established disciplines. In history it has been reflected in the rapid growth of interest in social and intellectual movements rather than political history. Literary studies began to move away from the formalist analysis familiar as the dominant mode of criticism during the 1940s and 1950s. At the same time there has been an increasing emphasis on continuity of ideas, contexts of ideology, and patterns of thought as "holistic" approaches to the comprehension of artistic, social, and intellectual movements. Discontent with compartmentalization in established disciplines has been accompanied by dissatisfaction with accepted methodological precepts which were inadequate for the understanding of the total range of American life. There has been a growing demand for a new methodological dimension: a cultural gestalt. The response to this excitement has been a lively dialogue among a group of scholars deeply committed to "American Studies" rather than to any single traditional discipline. Although they have differed in their conclusions concerning the possibility of developing a systematic methodology, they have not despaired of the original goal to study American culture systematically as a whole and yet do justice to its individual facets.

The work of scholars attracted to the American Studies ideal has been remarkable. A series of articles and books have been written which have injected new energy into the study of the history of American ideas, an area which had been limited to social, political, or economic thought with too little tolerance or understanding of the almost infinite complexities of literature or of the fine analytic techniques developed by the literary critics who have been interested in literature as literature.

The four writers whose work will be studied here have each contributed in some way to the debate over methodology. Moreover, each has written a book which exhibits strikingly the author's methodological position, so that studied together their work is highly revealing of the present conceptual apparatus of American Studies as a discipline. Each of these men comes to his discipline with a healthy concern for the underlying issue: whether the sphere of moral and imaginative values is in fact autonomous or dynamically related to culture. The broad methodological assumption of each is what we call holism. A more specific analytic concept each uses is myth. As a tool of analysis, mythopoesis in general is assumed by all to have a relationship to culture which renders the study of myths extremely valuable to historians of culture. The concept of the nature, inception, and growth of myth is similar in the theoretical framework of each of these writers and is directly dependent upon the concept of holism shared by all four. Other writers could equally well have been added but my intention was not to survey the holistic canon but to construct a model for analysis.

The plan of the book is to explore holism and myth in the contexts of each author's theoretical framework. Pearce, Smith, Ward, and Lewis are explicit about their methods in a very limited way, usually providing a few comments in the introduction to each book. Thus it will be necessary to extrapolate from the books themselves (and from the authors' articles, where relevant) the methodological concepts upon which each work stands. We will see how each writer develops and uses holism and myth and will examine both the similarities and the dissimilarities among them. However, the discussion will not be restricted to these two concepts. Each book will be viewed in the light of its own aims and its accomplishments, as well as the problems raised by the methods employed. In making this study I have gone far beyond the explicit statements of some of the authors, but not so far, I trust, that they will fail to recognize the intellectual and emotional substance of their writing.

A word about the organization of this book. After an introduction to holism and myth as general concepts, *The Continuity of American Poetry* is discussed in detail first, although published last, because it presents the most complex theoretical problems and contains the most systematic methodology. Its structure forms an excellent backdrop against which the other works may be seen. The pattern of discussion in each of the chapters on the individual volumes is similar. Then with chapter VI, I turn to the broader and more serious problems of holism, which make it impossible to accept in total the holistic canon: the concept of organicism, the uncritical concept of national character, and the consequences of literary nationalism. On the other hand, the important contributions of the holistic writers must surely be salvaged: their deep concern with and insight into the problem of the relationship of language to culture, their response to the New Critics' theory of language, and finally their profound attempt to return the study of moral and aesthetic values to their natural setting of the world we live and die in. All these issues are closely related to organic holism as a methodological assumption. Finally in chapter VII my concern is with the general problem of method itself and what some writers have called the "crisis in American Studies." I propose as an alternative to organic holism a "structural" approach to American Studies, for it seems to me that we have most to learn from structural anthropology and linguistics, which once again have raised the possibility of the unity of knowledge.

I
Holism and Myth in American Studies

Holism

When Tremaine McDowell's little book — *American Studies* — appeared in 1948, the American Studies movement was in its infancy.[1] But this publishing event set off a flurry of discussion, which has not yet ceased, about the possibility of a systematic method for American Studies. Since 1948 the debate has been carried on largely in academic journals. The issue joined in the journals was the extent to which a synoptic method could be agreed upon which viewed culture as a whole. The most cautious expectations were voiced by Henry Nash Smith. In "Can 'American Studies' Develop a Method?" — a key article published in 1957 — Smith states, "I do not imagine that a new method can be deduced from philosophical premises. A new method will have to come piecemeal, through a kind of principled opportunism, in the course of daily struggles with our various tasks."[2] But, Smith argues in a more optimistic mood, the desire which underlies American Studies is to analyze American culture as a whole and the desire validates the search for a method to implement such a study. Smith's cautious optimism may be compared with a view described by Robert E. Spiller. According to Spiller, the desire for a single method "for research in American Studies springs from the desire to find an *organic unity in the subject itself.*" He contrasts this view with one he attributes to older scholars like McDowell, who looked instead for "a synthesis in the mind of the student."[3]

9

Still another perspective is that of Richard Huber, who sees the search for a unified method as the reflection of a "general tendency" of ideas already present in American thought, ideas which "stress the importance of looking at reality as a whole, of analyzing the functional inter-relationships between the parts within the whole." This tendency is to be seen in many areas of thought: "organic architecture, functionalism in anthropology, gestalt psychology, holistic or heterodox economics, and to some extent cultural history."[4]

The views of Smith, Spiller, and Huber differ in their measure of optimism about the possibility of arriving at a methodology for American Studies. But the significant difference between them is rather of kind than of degree. Spiller's and Huber's "organic unity" is far removed from either Smith's "piecemeal" yet "principled opportunism" or McDowell's unity in the mind of the student. What Spiller describes is not a method which operates *as if* culture is a whole for the sake of gaining new insights and a synoptic view of man and his world, but one which believes that culture *is* a whole and reflects this perception procedurally.

What Spiller implies that some scholars desire, Roy Harvey Pearce hopes to fulfill. He urges first of all that the name "American Studies" be changed to "American Civilization" because the latter entails, not simply suggests, "some integrated genuinely holistic view of the phenomenon." Insisting, with Huber, on the importance of ideas from Gestalt psychology, holistic economics, and functional anthropology as integrating principles for American Studies, he presupposes that American civilization is a functioning whole. He then argues that although American Studies has not yet achieved the status of a discipline, it most certainly can and should, and "the form of our discipline ... must reflect our sense of the wholeness of our civilization."[5] He assumes, first, that the "form" of the discipline must reflect the "form" of the object of study, and, second, that the form of this object — American Civilization — is organic.* Pearce calls what emerges from the

---

*One of the recurring problems in American Studies is whether or not there is any empirical evidence to support these two assumptions. The second assumption is especially troublesome and one of the goals of my study is to work out the logical implications of organic holism, in its strong sense, to show that it is unacceptable for a theoretical grounding of American Studies.

activity in American Studies "a functionalist mode of literary analysis." "Its practitioners strive to see in what way, and to what effect, and for what value, a literary work is an 'expression' of the civilization out of which it comes. Doing so, they begin to bring literature as an expression into focus with other modes. . . . And then it will indeed be possible for American Civilization to be a discipline . . . within . . . the 'holistic' study of civilization."[6]

The belief upon which the methodological thinking of a large segment of American Studies is grounded I shall call, along with Pearce, "holistic." *The American Adam, The Continuity of American Poetry, Virgin Land,* and *Andrew Jackson, Symbol for an Age,* along with many other studies of American culture, all make some kind of holistic assumption about the nature of culture.

Holism is first of all a belief about the nature of culture. Traditionally it means simply that there are such things as identifiable cultural units. The "unit" is not a mere abstraction, but something which exists prior to, and independently of, the cognitive activity of the human mind. It simply *is* as a part of reality. Hence, if holism is true, the cultural unit is a proper object for study as a whole. The social sciences have long led the way in seeking the adoption of a holistic assumption upon which to establish a method of study. In anthropology this search has resulted in an analogy between culture and human personality. Robert Redfield argues that "a culture or a personality is 'known' . . . by an effort of comprehension which is not analytic, which insists on a view of the whole as a whole." Redfield deplores what he believes are the futile attempts of some social scientists to represent a culture "by a list, a formula of structural relationships." These are false starts toward understanding cultural reality and must be corrected "by the insistence of the reality itself which is so much more than any of these. This 'more' is the whole apprehended without resolution into elements."[7]

Many social psychologists have paralleled anthropologists in their approval of holism as a belief and in their use of the analogy between human personality and culture. W. E. Coutu asserts that "culture is to a population aggregate what personality is to the individual; and the ethos is to the culture what self is to a personality, the core of most probable behaviors." Thus "culture is one of the most inclusive of all the configurations we call interactional fields"; it is the way of life of a whole people like that of China or the United States.[8] By a simple extension of the analogy between culture and human personality suggested by Redfield, a definition of culture like Coutu's links the organic personality of an individual to the structural configurations of a national culture.

The second important aspect of holism is that a culture is conceived of as a functioning independent organism. This idea simply continues the analogy between culture and an individual man. Long ago the pioneer American sociologist Lester Frank Ward led the way when he said, "A culture is . . . a social organism . . . and ideas are its germs."[9] If a culture is an organism, as Ward asserts, it follows that like any other organism it has a life of its own. It must be subject to its own internal laws of birth, growth, and death; just like any other organism, it must be subject to fixed laws of change. But these laws are unique to each individual culture. They are not identifiable with the natural laws governing the people living in the culture any more than the laws which apply to the whole human being are applicable to the life process of a cell within the human body. Thus the anthropologist C. J. Warden can write, "Those patterns of group life which exist only by virtue of the operation of the three-fold mechanism — invention, communication, and social habitation — belong to the cultural order. . . . The cultural order is superorganic and possesses its own modes of operation and its own type of patterning."[10]

It requires only a minor extension of the original analogy to make the short step to the third important concept of holistic thinking: an organism has certain discernible patterns of behavior. A man undergoes change in accordance with biological laws governing the human species. Yet a man also exhibits continuity in the various forms of his existence, i.e., character, personality, appearance — all the things that go into making up what we might call the "style" of the man. It is a simple matter for anthropologists to extend this idea to a culture. To Meyer Schapiro, "Style is . . . the constant form — and sometimes the constant elements, qualities, and expression — in the art of an individual or a group. The term is also applied to the whole activity of an individual or society, as in speaking of a 'life style' or the 'style' of a civilization."[11]

So far three important aspects of holistic thinking have been isolated:

1. A culture is more than the mere sum of its members and therefore must be viewed as whole.
2. A culture is a functioning independent structure like an organism, exhibiting many of the characteristics of human personality and life.
3. Like an organism, a culture exhibits identifiable continuities or themes. Anthropologists refer to these continuities as the style of the culture. A style reflects the organic structure of a culture just as a personality reflects a whole human being. In a similar manner the internal development of a culture is reflected in the style of all its various aspects: social and political institutions, religion, art, philosophy, and literature and consequently in all the ideas, beliefs, and attitudes of individuals. A culture, in other words, has a character of its own.

From these characteristics, holistic thinkers deduce many others, two of which are important for this study:

1. As an organic functioning whole, a culture's inner process is dynamic and extrapersonal. Human behavior, and consequently all historical or social change, is viewed as a consequence of a nonhuman agency. Some impersonal force is often posited to account for change.* This impersonal force according to Leslie A. White is the culture itself: "The culturologist explains the behavior of the human organism in terms of external, extrasomatic cultural elements that function as stimuli to evoke the response and give it a form and content." In addition, "the culturologist knows also that the culture process is explainable in terms of itself; the human organism is irrelevant — not to the culture process itself — but to an explanation of the culture process."[12] In this view the extrasomatic continuum of cultural events is not the same thing at all as a class of human organisms considered individually or collectively; nor is the interaction of cultural events identifiable with a class of reactions or interactions of human organisms. This is an extreme statement of the nature of extrapersonal social forces of change, but it illustrates well a concept that is important in holistic thought.

*Marxism, one form of holism, emphasizes economic forces as the sole dynamic of change.

2. If a culture is a whole, like an organism it is unique. By the very complexity of its history, it is absolutely single. As Roy Harvey Pearce puts it, "What has eventuated is unique; and it is the recording, comprehending, and evaluating of that uniqueness toward which we must strive."[13]

These characteristics do not constitute a definition of holism but rather an anatomical description of some of its chief aspects. For holism is a set of beliefs, a canon of assumptions, a collection of attitudes, rather than a theory. In setting up the canon and outlining its consequences, I have attempted to make the case for holism as strong as possible without excessive qualification and criticism. Problems will be obvious to many readers, and at least some of these problems will be the major focus of the latter parts of the book. Here it is enough to emphasize that holistic beliefs often underlie cultural theories.

What, then, of the holistic perspective of American Studies? The following statements are taken from *The American Adam*, where Lewis is seeking some identifiable feature of American culture:

> *Leaves of Grass* . . . brought to its climax the many-sided discussion by which — over a generation — innocence replaced sinfulness as the first attribute of the American character.

> My intention, then, is to disentangle from the writings and pronouncements of the day the emergent American myth and the dialogue in which it was formed. The American myth . . . was not fashioned . . . by a single man of genius. It was and it has remained a collective affair.

> . . . the debate in turn can contribute to the shaping of the story; and when the results of rational inquiry are transformed into conscious and coherent narrative by the best-attuned artists of the time, the culture has finally yielded up its own special and identifying "myth."[14]

Lewis's first statement emphasizes the notion of an American cultural or national character, the second, the notion of a pattern which is collective, identifying, and cultural; the third statement stresses the relationship of art to the inner process and development of the culture as a whole. In the second and third statements it is significant, for our later discussion, that Lewis uses the word *myth* to suggest the pattern he is seeking to identify.

In his article "Can 'American Studies' Develop a Method?" Henry Nash Smith expressed a conservative but hopeful belief that a holistic approach to culture would bear fruit. *Virgin Land* sustains that belief, for its framework is holistic in the full sense rather than in the merely methodological or "as if" sense of holism. Holism underlies the author's concepts of myth and symbol as cultural phenomena. Myth and symbol are interpreted as organic and unconscious outgrowths of the culture itself, created as human beings interact with the culture and with each other. Defining the terms he will be using, Smith says: "I use the words [*myth* and *symbol*] to designate larger or smaller units of the same kind of thing, namely an intellectual construction that fuses concept and emotion into an image. The myths and symbols with which I deal have the further characteristic of being collective representations rather than the work of a single mind."[15] The myths and symbols which Smith calls "collective representations" may be designated "creations of the time."[16] They are believed in by a large number (perhaps most) of the people in a culture at a given time. An example would be the myth Smith calls the "garden of the world." By studying such a myth, we should be able to learn a great deal about the whole culture. The real importance of the idea of the garden of the world to a historian is that it was an expression of "the assumptions and aspirations of a whole society."[17]

Following the lead of his teacher, Henry Nash Smith, John William Ward in *Andrew Jackson, Symbol for an Age* argues that "the symbolic Andrew Jackson is the creation of his time. Through the age's leading figure were projected the age's leading ideas." These ideas, "nature, providence, and will, are organically inter-related; they possess a logical coherence which makes a whole."[18] It is clear by now that "myth" and "symbol," as the terms are used by Lewis, Smith, and Ward, are not conscious constructs of individuals in the culture. They are unconscious outgrowths reflecting deeper-lying, nonrational patterns of the culture.*

*As we will see, although myths begin as unconscious constructs, they may become conscious as they develop. See especially chapters III and V below. Both Smith and Lewis suggest that cultural myths become conscious in the latter stages of their development. Smith argues that sometimes people may be manipulated by deliberate exploitation of myths. Lewis believes that myths emerge gradually and become an issue for debate.

Of the four writers whose work is under review here, Roy Harvey Pearce is the most holistically oriented. *The Continuity of American Poetry* exhibits a thorough cultural holism in his theories of language and art: "The poet's particular relation to his culture – his self-imposed obligation to make the best possible use of the language he is given – is such as to put him at the center of the web of communications which gives his culture its characteristic style and spirit."[19] The concept of a cultural style is employed by Pearce with reference to language and the function of poetry, once again confirming his holistic orientation. According to Pearce, the "style" of a culture should give the student insight into the inner processes of the culture as a whole. This insight, he argues, will place the student in a privileged position so that he may write what Pearce calls an "inside narrative" of a culture. And "an inside narrative must have its proper ambiance," which in Pearce's study "is the general cultural style of a poet's age as it is at once the background against which and the ground out of which he works."[20]

All of the works examined in this book share specific holistic assumptions. Many of these are analyzed in the chapters dealing with each work. However, the most important assumption they all share is a particular concept of myth and it is to that concept that we must turn now in order to understand its importance to contemporary studies of American culture.

Myth

Holism is a belief about the nature of culture. It is not in itself a methodology or a tool for understanding. Instead, it prescribes what a methodology – a tool – must be like if understanding is to be achieved. Holism dictates that in analyzing the structure and functioning of a culture, the cultural historian should make use of the principle of organic wholeness. According to this principle, no part of the culture can be fully understood except in its interrelatedness with other parts. Each aspect of the culture, its literature or its philosophy, its political or its religious institutions, must therefore be analyzed within the context of the cultural whole in which it is rooted.

Besides the principle of organic wholeness, the cultural historian who accepts the holistic position must make use of the notion of cultural development. Since the cultural organism has a life, a history — a past, a present, and a future — the historian will find it essential to inquire into the dynamic factors of cultural change and growth, and to consider the pattern of that growth.

Holism insists that the particular tool used for understanding must, therefore, be one with which an investigator can apprehend, first, the complex functioning of the unique cultural unit in its organic inter-relationship and, second, the patterns of development of the cultural unit in relation to its past, which in part constitutes it, and its present — its existence now. Holism, however, does not appear to imply that one specific method is the sole valid tool for the implementation of the kind of investigation that is desired.

The approach which American Studies has developed over the last two decades is one which places a heavy emphasis on myth as a key to the understanding of culture. Since Frazer's classic, *The Golden Bough*, the study of mythopoesis has gained in stature until it constitutes a separate branch of ethnology. Not only anthropologists but also psychologists and philosophers have had a great deal to say about myth, its origin, its function, and its meaning. None of the writers in whom we are interested here is a mythologist concerned with the speculative origins of myth. Nevertheless they are concerned, however indirectly, with the theoretical origin, function, and meaning of myth within a cultural context. Pearce, Smith, Ward, and Lewis all have some rather firm convictions about the relationship of myth to culture. This rela-tionship, as we will see, is specifically presupposed by their holistic orientation. These convictions are a consequence of several important developments in the study of myth since Frazer, which have contrib-uted to its usefulness as a methodological tool for understanding the phenomenon of a culture.

Clearly myth conceived of simply as false belief is an insufficient conception, and as a tool for American Studies it has no value. Yet it is a popular and widespread concept which has remained difficult to overcome. This meaning of myth is found in popular essays and in a large amount of social and political criticism. It is the meaning implied by all suggestions that we should somehow distinguish between "truth" and "myth."

Neither Pearce, Smith, Ward, nor Lewis views myth simply as self-delusion. For the most part, they are neutral with respect to judgments of correspondence between myth and reality. This suspended judgment is reflected in Smith's comment: "I do not mean to raise the question whether such products [myths] of the imagination accurately reflect empirical fact. They exist on a different plane. But," he goes on to say, ". . . they sometimes exert a decided influence on practical affairs."[21] Pearce, Ward, and Lewis as well as Smith view myth as in some degree causal and dynamic. For example, Pearce uses the term *impulse* to describe the mythic theme in American poetry which he calls "Adamic." He conceives of the "Adamic impulse" as a force, below the conscious level of reality, which has historically directed American poetry into discoverable patterns.[22]

Two developments which have been particularly stimulating to scholars interested in the study of culture have been the psychosymbolic and the cognitive concepts of myth. The first major development may be traced to the influence of Freud, who argued that dreams symbolize what lies beneath the conscious level of man's mental life. In the context of Freud's psychoanalytic theory, myths, like dreams, are symbolic. The symbolic value of myth is closely tied to its function, which is to reflect a level of reality that is psychological and ethnohistorical. Myths symbolize reality in that, like dreams, they are a form of "wish-fulfillment." Myth is also, like dreaming, regressive, and its significance is determined by the genetic and ethnohistorical experiences of the individual and the race. In *Totem and Taboo*, Freud fused a symbolic interpretation of the Oedipus myth with the suggestion of Darwin and others that the original state in which man lived was as a member of a "primal horde." The slaying of the tyrannical, repressive father by the sons was commemorated by primitive man in the totem feast which marked the beginning of social organization, moral restrictions, and religion.[23]

The specific content of Freud's theory of myth is not nearly so important as his emphasis on the unconscious origins of myth and its symbolic reference to a nonempirical level of reality. With modification, this idea has been useful in the study of culture. It is in complete accord with the holistic emphasis on the way in which cultural forms reflect the inner, nonempirical, organic level of cultural reality. Myth, however, conceived as simply one cultural form among many is no more nor less important a tool for cultural analysis than any other cultural form.

However, a second line of thinking has contributed immeasurably to the idea that myth is singularly important as a methodological tool for analysis. The theory that has come to us from philosophical anthropology began with Kant and was developed systematically by Ernst Cassirer. To Cassirer, myth is the primary cognitive form under which all reality is viewed. Mythological thinking is the most fundamental and therefore most pervasive level of consciousness. Following Kant, Cassirer suggests that all knowledge involves, at the instant of its perception, a synthesizing activity of the mind. Mythic thinking, as the most basic kind of synthetic activity which the mind performs, is the way man organizes all of his experience initially.[24] The chief limitation of this theory of myth is the assumption it requires one to make that mythopoesis is involved in the very act of perception itself. This completely neglects the narrative content of myth as well as its close relationship to religion.

The important contribution of Cassirer's thought, however, has been the concept of myth as a form under which reality appears and takes on the shape which is inherent in the form. This idea, if connected with the holistic point that myth emerges from and reflects the inner workings of the culture itself, implies that individuals in that culture unit will view reality under the aspect of an emergent cultural form. This does not necessarily imply, however, as does Cassirer's theory, that mythopoesis is involved in the very act of perception, but rather recognizes that reality is interpreted in different ways depending upon *which lens* is involved.

For the concept of myth that has proven most useful to American Studies, we must turn once again to social scientists who, having borrowed from both the psychologists and the philosophers, have added ideas and concepts of their own:

> By *myths* we mean the value-impregnated beliefs and notions
> that men hold, that they live by or live for. Every society is held
> together by . . . a complex of dominating thought-forms that

determines and sustains all its activities. All social relations, the very texture of human society, are myth-born and myth-sustained. . . . We use the word [myth] in an entirely neutral sense. Whether its content be revelation or superstition, insight or prejudice, is not here in question. . . . We include equally under the term "myth" the most penetrating philosophies of life, the most profound intimations of religion, the most subtle renditions of experience. . . . Whatever valuational responses men give to the circumstances and trials of their lot, whatever conceptions guide their behavior, spur their ambitions, or render existence tolerable — all alike fall within [the] category of myth.[25]

This passage from Robert M. MacIver's *The Web of Government* relates, in a new way, those lessons learned from the psychological and cognitive theories so that they form a broad base upon which to build a science of culture. MacIver suspends any judgment upon the truth or falsity of myths — the term itself is "neutral." This concept of myths as dominating thought forms, which shape reality as they emerge from the society, is close to Cassirer's epistemological lens through which reality appears. Again, as in the psychocultural concept, myths are culturally emergent forms. They are not the creations of individuals but spring from the nonrational, nonpersonal level of culture. To these basic ideas, MacIver has added two more: the notion of the indissoluble relationship between myths and the wholeness of a culture; and the notion that myths are instrumental in sustaining the very life of the culture.

This synthesis of ideas furnishes the basis from which American Studies has developed myth as a tool for the holistic analysis of culture. Myths are the social adhesive, the ideological glue, which holds a society together as a functioning whole.* The "texture" of society, as MacIver states, is "myth-born" and "myth-sustained." In other words, myths are the instrumental means by which society satisfies its needs, sustains its existence, and enhances its growth.

Returning to the analogy between the human organism and the cultural organism, we may usefully remind ourselves of John Dewey's comments on the self-sustaining adjustment of the human being to his environment. According to Dewey, the existence and growth of the

---

*I shall use the term *ideology*, as MacIver does, to mean simply any pattern of thinking characteristic of a group or class. See *The Web of Government*, p. 339.

human organism are determined by the functional relation between what Dewey calls "habit" and the environment.[26] "Habits" are arts, ideas, cunning, or craft — in other words, those instruments of behavior which provide the organism with stasis and a release from the tension and conflict which threaten the organism's balance and pattern of existence. If we substitute the terms *myth* for *habit* and *cultural organism* for *human organism*, we have a good idea of MacIver's meaning. Myths include all valuational or ideological thought whatsoever, and MacIver is interested in myth and in the cultural matrix from which myth grows and which it in turn reinforces.

The work of social psychologist Kimball Young, like that of MacIver, emphasizes the instrumental and ideological character of myth. "The most significant myths and legends," Young declares, "emerge out of recurrent problems of adjustment of our physical and social-cultural world."[27] As MacIver and Young understand myth, it is inextricably involved with culture; myths are determined almost wholly by the culture out of which they emerge and are in turn the pragmatic instruments for cultural development and adjustment. Writing of primitive culture, Bronislaw Malinowski points out: "Myth fulfills in primitive culture an indispensable function: it expresses, enhances, and codifies belief; it safeguards and enforces morality; it vouches for the efficiency of ritual and contains practical rules for the guidance of man. Myth is thus a vital ingredient of human civilization; it is not an idle tale, but a hard-worked active force; it is not an intellectual explanation or an artistic imagery, but a pragmatic charter of primitive faith and moral wisdom."[28] Malinowski, while emphasizing the pragmatic aspect of mythopoesis, also stresses its universality and "vital" necessity to all civilization.

Clearly, the social sciences have established a broad base upon which to build a study of a culture as a whole through the emergent forms of its dominant ideologies or myths. However, the view of myth typified by MacIver requires one final development before it can be considered a useful concept for American Studies. We should remember that Pearce, Smith, Ward, and Lewis are deeply interested in literature and popular art and are particularly sensitive to the representational or narrative aspects of myth in its traditional form as tales of heroes and gods.

MacIver's concept of ideological "thought forms," like Cassirer's concept of cognitive synthesis, leaves out the narrative content of myth entirely. What connection then, if any, can be made between ideology or the "dominant thought forms" which are "pragmatic charters" for cultural existence and the ancient form of myth as stories and tales of the deeds and quests of gods and heroes?

To make this final connection, American Studies has both borrowed from and added to work by social scientists. A specific illustration of this point will help to clarify it further. The anthropologist Leslie White argues that in order to understand the culture hero, we must understand the function he performs in relation to his culture.

> In history, in political and social movements, the Great Man is that anatomical part of a social organism that functions as a directive, regulative or integrative mechanism. . . . The [hero] is an instrument employed by a nation or a movement in the exercise of its functions. . . . The measure of a [hero] in the life of nations can be taken when we see how independent of him the behavior of a nation is. The behavior of the social organism that is Russia has remained constant for decades and even centuries. . . . Whether a Czar or a Commissar sits in the driver's seat is immaterial; the great organism goes its own way unalterably. . . . [T]he behavior of the social organism remains constant. The [hero] is the instrument, the Ideology, the rationalization, of the social organism. . . .[29]

But surely the hero is not *identical* with the ideology of the society as White states; on the other hand, the thrust of White's argument is that in some sense the hero *embodies* the ideology. This is precisely the view shared by Pearce, Smith, Ward, and Lewis: the culture hero embodies the ideological or valuational preoccupations of the culture in a mythological form which has definite narrative content.

When Pearce speaks of the "basic styles" of a culture, he means essentially the same kind of thing as does MacIver in his description of "thought forms." A "general cultural style," says Pearce, is "expressive of the life of [a] community."[30] There exist "shared communal assumptions, conscious and unconscious," which spring from the "general style" of the whole culture. Within the ambience of the "general style," growing out of it and reflecting it, are the numerous "basic styles" belonging to the various aspects of the culture (philosophy, social theory, religion, and the like). The basic style invests the poet's individual style with its character.

But in Pearce, unlike MacIver, the most significant feature of the basic style is that it is embodied in the Adamic image and thus has assumed a representational character with a strong narrative element. Indeed, it is the "Adamic impulse," according to Pearce, which is the dynamic mythic force that reflects the egocentric, individualistic ideology of American culture.

In *Virgin Land* the idea of the West held by Americans is similar to a "dominant thought form" described by MacIver. But there is an important difference. The myths that formed about the West (the "passage to India" and the "garden of the world") are "collective representations," according to Smith, which embody the aspirations of the American people in the nineteenth century. These "collective representations" have both symbolic significance and narrative content. Again in *Andrew Jackson, Symbol for an Age* the symbolic Andrew Jackson condenses a number of ideas into a dramatic image. The symbol, the hero, embodies in his own person the ideological commitments of his culture.

Finally, Lewis also refines the view derived from MacIver and the social sciences. A society produces a debate in its literature and thought which is inseparable from the society's primary ideological concerns. The mythic image which represented the preoccupations of the debate in the nineteenth century was the "American Adam." Lewis, along with Pearce, Smith, and Ward, implies that ideology springs from the preoccupations of a culture and that ideology is crystallized by a mythic embodiment of the ideological themes.

The refinements added by Pearce, Smith, Ward, and Lewis constitute a methodological advance over the MacIver view because the term *myth* is used by MacIver as simply synonymous with *thought forms* while *myth* is used by Pearce, Smith, Ward, and Lewis to *describe* "dominant thought forms" as they become embodied in a particular image or complex of images. An analysis of the image and of stories with strong mythical content provides a method for the study of culture, suited particularly to revealing the inner dynamics of culture as a holistic phenomenon.

The social sciences have taught that culture is a closely knit, highly complex whole; it is organistic and dynamically interrelated — each change, each development has effects throughout. According to this view every pattern of ideas, vision of reality, or system of ethics, every institutional structure of social control — in other words, each embodiment of the belief and ideology that pragmatically charters the total cultural entity — both reflects and affects the total culture. The pragmatic charter which interests us here is myth in its traditional sense: symbolic and narrative. As American Studies understands myths, they are inextricably involved with a particular national culture, a whole culture, from which they emerge and whose "dominant thought forms" they body forth with imaginative impact. Whether or not we agree with this vision of culture, it has had a decisive impact on the development of American Studies.

The two methodological areas of interest in American Studies today discussed in this chapter are closely related to each other. Yet the way in which each writer reviewed here has used the concepts we have been examining has been largely a personal matter. A holistic orientation does not necessarily dictate the exact tool to be used for cultural analysis nor does it dictate the exact way in which a specific tool, such as myth, is to be used for interpreting cultural phenomena. Our next task, then, is to examine the works of Pearce, Smith, Ward, and Lewis individually to see both how the holistic orientation of each of these writers is reflected in his analyses and how it affects his use of myth.

II

The Poet as a Culture Hero: Pearce's *The Continuity of American Poetry*

The Conceptual Framework: The Unity of Poetry, Language, and Culture

In *The Continuity of American Poetry* (1961), Roy Harvey Pearce sets for himself a comprehensive critical task: to discover a unifying principle in American poetry from the Puritan writers to the present and in so doing to illustrate a theory which systematically relates American poetry to American culture. He proposes to base his findings on a close critical reading and textual explication. The results are often excellent. Pearce is committed to the search for a unity in American poetry, yet throughout the text he is also dedicated to pointing out diversity and singularity among individual poets. He seldom shirks detailed analysis, the critic's first duty to his readers. Moreover, once the reader has mastered the author's gnarled style, he begins to see that what Pearce is engaged in developing is indeed serious; it is nothing less than a theory of the relationship of poetry, language, and culture.

The social sciences have furnished a theoretical background for Pearce. Over the past twenty-five years cultural anthropologists and linguists have slowly moved from an atomistic definition of culture, which described it as a fairly haphazard collection of traits, to a definition which emphasizes interrelationships and large patterns or configurations. Along with this new understanding of the nature of culture taken as a whole, there has also developed a new conception of the relationship between language and culture. Language, once thought of as totally distinct from other aspects of a culture, now is conceived of as part of the whole and as functionally related to it. The conception of language which has developed along with the holistic view of culture places language at the dynamic center of culture. Describing this relationship, Harry Hoijer argues that "it is quite impossible to conceive of either the origin or the development of culture apart from language, for language is that part of culture which, more than any other, enables men not only to make their own experiences and learning continuous but, as well, to participate vicariously in the experience and learning of others. . . . To the extent that a culture as a whole is made up of common understanding, its linguistic aspect is its most vital and necessary part."[1] The holistic concept of culture, along with the emphasis on the functional centrality of language, is indispensable to Pearce, for from it he develops his theory of the relationship of the poet to his culture.

In a densely packed "Foreword" Pearce sets up his conceptual framework. Like F. O. Matthiessen in *American Renaissance*, he believes that the poet's place in a culture is central. He explains the relationship with a brief formula — poet: language: culture.* What does he mean? If, as social scientists maintain, language is central and interpenetrates all cultural phenomena, then it is the essential carrier of culture. The implication of this view is that language is, at all times, the most sensitive index of a culture — its rhythms and patterns, and thus, perforce, its "style." Pearce affirms this conception in his own view. It is but a short step to his belief in the poet's importance in the life of a culture. Since the poet is the most sensitive user of language, he is literally at the very center of a culture. By virtue of his unique relationship to language, he is inevitably more aware than others of cultural

---

*Matthiessen seems to have been the immediate source of this formula. In *American Renaissance* (New York, 1941, p. xv) Matthiessen states: "An artist's use of language is the most sensitive index to cultural history, since a man can only articulate what he is, and what he has been made by the society of which he is a willing or unwilling part."

patterns, rhythms, tensions, ambiguities, and strains. Hence, poet: language: culture.

The poet's position in culture suggests that a history of poetry (if written with attention to the poet's cultural awareness) is an "inside narrative." By inside narrative, Pearce means "what Melville meant when he applied the term to *Billy Budd*: a story of the life-sustaining tension between commitments and results, aspirations and accomplishments, theory and practice."[2] In Pearce's view, phenomena such as cultural tensions and commitments will be reflected in the poet's work as a result of his singular position. A historian who is himself sensitive and who pays close attention to the embodiment of culture in poetry will be in a position to write a narrative from the "inside": one that reveals the inner dynamics of the cultural organism.

Moreover, because of the poet's special use of language, his poetry gains vitality, not from his own life and inspiration alone, but also from his cultural environment. Indeed, argues Pearce, poetry has "life only *in* a world." That world, or poetic ambience, is the general "style" of the culture of the poet's age; it is the background against which he must work and the source from which his vital materials come.[3]

The concept of cultural style is familiar to us from the discussion in chapter I, but Pearce has adapted it to the needs of his theory of poetry and culture. Pearce is interested in a poem's particularity; that is, he wants to show how a poet orders a poem "in and of itself." But he also wants to show how a poem is ordered "in relation to the culture out of which it comes." The thrust of his argument is from the particular to the general, from the poem to the culture. "I have insisted," writes Pearce, "that it is possible to move from a sense of the individual style of a poem . . . to that of its culture. Indeed, I have tried to show how the works of our great poets cluster around a series of 'basic' poetic styles. . . ."[4] These basic styles are to be understood as they "articulate" with other basic cultural styles in art, philosophy, religion, social theory, and so on. The basic styles, fully articulated, make up the "general" style of the culture.

We have, then, distinguished three levels of styles: the particular style of the poet's poem or poems; the basic poetic style from which the poem issues and which mediates between the poem and the general style; and the general style of the culture as a whole. The task Pearce sets for himself is to discuss all three levels, thereby illustrating his theory in action.

The author's first concern is to give a close analysis of the work of individual poets against the background of the immediate poetic ambience. The poetic ambience (the basic style) is made up of the "communal assumptions, conscious and unconscious," which make composition possible, as well as the tensions, aspirations, and commitments which are reflected in the poetry. Ultimately "the poet's relation to his culture's general life-style and to the basic poetic style which mediates between it and his own style" is a complex one; the basic style is "the grammar and syntax of the sensibility as it is given to a poet to extend and deepen and so accommodate to his sense of the possibilities . . . for living life fully in his culture."[5]

The individuality of a poet's style is therefore only a "unique variation" upon the basic style. It is the basic poetic style of a period which makes poetry possible at all. "For, as it is expressive of the life of his community, it gives [the poet] the terms in which he may work toward his own unique style. Basic style — as mode and strategy, as pattern and plan-of-attack — is a necessary condition of artistic creation."[6] In one sense, the poet moves in a direction precisely opposite that of the historian. That is, the poet moves from his sense of the basic style out of which he works to a personal style, while the historian's task is to study particular poems and their styles and to generalize about the basic style of the culture from his investigation. Ultimately, of course, the historian will want to infer even more general conclusions about the life style of the culture, based upon his understanding of the basic style.

Pearce acknowledges the great difficulty of working with the idea of cultural styles, which, after all, are not expressed with the grace and felicity of particular poetic styles. The question is, to what extent is a style an active determining force? As we shall see, Pearce is ambivalent on what the answer is. He insists basic style can never be found in one poem or even in the entire body of a poet's work. But it is implied, and tacitly contained there, even as it is latent in the life of the culture. The historian, realizing this, also realizes that the basic style exists ideally only as a historical construct.

The construct must be filled out as the historian works back from the individual poems, which are necessarily bound to the life of the culture through the basic style. Once this is done, he (or his readers) can see the "determining immanence" of the basic style. Thus, although the historian moves from the particular to the general (specific poem to the basic style), this does not mean that the basic style is simply a generalization or abstraction.

There are, then, two aspects of basic style in Pearce's discussion that should be distinguished. When he calls basic style a historical construct, Pearce means that it is a typology or model which exists in a pure state only in the mind of the historian. On the other hand, basic style is not simply the term for an ideal type. He assumes that it has a causal relationship, in some sense, to individual poetic style. It is "in part at least ... determinative. It prescribes a direction in which the poet's imagination may move; it delimits the areas of experience on which his sensibility may be operative; and it supplies his mind with a 'content' — a substance of motifs, conceptions, and the like. . . ."[7]

It is through the mediation of the basic style that the poet's unique style reaches his readers. The poet's relationship to his readers is, as we shall see, a heroic one. It is enough to say here that great poetry necessarily informs human beings of the possibilities of moral choice inherent in men, as these possibilities are circumscribed by the cultural ambience. Accordingly, Pearce argues, "solving problems in the composition of poetry, he [the poet] teaches his readers to pose problems in the composition of their lives ... teaches them to define their life-styles."[8] The basic style of a period is a communal thing, shared by all members of a culture; it is the very thing, in fact, which makes poetry the viable vehicle that it is for the subtlest forms of communication. The history of American poetry is the history of a series of basic styles which furnished the poets the necessary elements for the realization of their individual talents. To write this history that Pearce envisions is at once to comprehend poetry as the deepest expression of the life of the culture and to comprehend the life of the culture in its richest fusion with the particularity of the poetry.

Pearce's Use of Myth: The Poet and
the Culture Hero Myth

One of Pearce's principal hopes is to illustrate the relationship between poetry and the values of the culture which gives it life, and hence to bridge the gap made by the New Critics between literature and its historical and cultural origins.

According to Pearce, the poet is both a conservator and an innovator with respect to values. This dualism means in part what Eliot means when he argues that the poet creates something new but always within a particular tradition which he is interested in preserving. But for the American poet it means more, for, as Pearce insists, the American poet had no native tradition from which to work. He first had to create a tradition and this is one of the unique characteristics of American poetry.[9]

As we have seen, the poet is in an extraordinary position "at the center of the web of communications," which invests his culture with its style and colors its spirit. The inevitably sensitive process of his acculturation imparts to him the structural aspects, ideological as well as artistic, of the culture. Part of the basic style from which his material must be drawn will necessarily be the dominant values of the culture. The poet's relationship to language once again defines his uniqueness: "For, above all in poetry, language transmits *values*: an awareness of the infinite degree of choice involved in being 'for' or 'against' something. . . . Poetry is thus a means whereby, through the imaginative use of language, we may be made aware of the values of a culture as they have (and have not) made possible the communal life of the individuals of whom it is composed."[10]

The transmission of values is, therefore, one of the major functions of poetry. Like the language of the moralist, the language of poetry concerns tradition. In Pearce's words, poetry is "compulsively traditional" in its role of preserving traditional values which have made life what it is within a culture.

Yet the poet, more than anyone else in a culture, raises the question of new directions. His language is creative, varied, and innovative. By virtue of being at the center of culture, he is the most sensitive respondent not only to tradition but also to cultural change and hence to the emergence of new values and the recasting of old values in new forms. This implies that the tension that exists between tradition and innovation as the culture evolves is reflected by a parallel tension in the poet's sensibility and hence in his poetry.

Tension in poetic language is simply a reflection of the dominant tensions in the culture involving conflicts between traditional values and new or emerging values. The poet's position forces him to attempt a creative resolution of the tensions which he finds in a culture. Poetry is language at the height of creative control; it is innovative but also conservative. The poet is "compulsively traditional" but also "compulsively modern."[11]

The problem of cultural tension and conflict of values leads to Pearce's conception of the epic, one of the unique aspects of his theory. He connects the cultural function of the traditional epic poem to the poet's universal cultural function. According to Pearce, the traditional epic celebrated a mythical, traditional cultural hero. The epic poet sought to embody within one poem the essence of the total culture, giving it "form, substance, and meaning."[12] Within the epic, cultural tensions and contradictions found their resolution. The epic poem became the mythic expression of a whole people and a whole culture.

But from the beginning American poets have faced an almost insuperable problem: the lack of a native tradition. This has prevented the writing of a genuine American epic and has pervaded the spirit of all major American poetry. When an American poet has attempted to write in the epic form, he has inevitably set for himself "an impossible task — writing an epic without the sort of linear, form-endowing narrative argument which takes its substance and its very life from the hero, the supra-human being, at its center."[13] He has been forced to attempt a unique solution. "The major theme of all epic poetry," Pearce quotes Stephen Gilman, "is heroism itself, heroism as the perilous mythification of man. . . ."[14] But American poets found no ready-made hero to celebrate: "[The American poet] was constitutionally the one in whom the latent antinomianism of his culture was most likely to erupt. Then how could he find the means — the source in some *numen*, some absolutely authoritative power — to discover and describe that culture hero required to make a proper epic? In what could the poet believe

... ? In whom could he believe except himself?"[15] Thus, although confronted by the absence of the traditional materials of epic poetry — a transcendent faith, tradition, and a ready-made hero, some of the greatest American poets have attempted desperately to work in something like the epic mode, most notably in such poems as *Song of Myself*, the *Cantos, The Bridge*, and *Paterson*. But all are plotless, and like their culture they have no proper traditional hero.

The lack of a traditional culture hero in the modern world is not unique to America. While describing the modern decay of cultural myth, Joseph Campbell says, "The problem of mankind today ... is precisely the opposite to that of men in the comparatively stable periods of those great co-ordinating mythologies." Indeed, in the past "all meaning was in the group ... none in the self-expressive individual; today no meaning is in the group — none in the world: all is in the individual."[16] If there is no meaning in the group, the poet must look inward for his meaning. The poet "looks at the world with reference to himself, and not at himself with reference to the world"; this is the true significance of the Adamic impulse in American poetry.[17]

The chief characteristic of the American epic is that it tries to create the missing hero and his history "rather than recall the history that surrounds him. In the American epic what is mythified is the total milieu and ambiance, what the poet takes to be the informing spirit of his times and his world."[18] If it were successful, a new epic form would emerge, one in which the poet has transformed his world and himself and in one desperate act has re-created the world with himself as its heroic center. "I celebrate myself, and sing myself, / And what I assume you shall assume, / For every atom belonging to me as good belongs to you."[19] The poet thus addresses the reader as he begins his epic. His intent is the traditional one of resolving cultural tension but he must create the hero. In order to do this, he must engage his reader in a process of transformation exactly parallel to his own so that the reader, in participating in the poet's heroic self-creation, is transformed and becomes himself the heroic center and hence one with his culture. Pearce's tone suggests again and again that the compulsive task the American poet has assumed is the most difficult that any poets of any

time have confronted. Pearce truly believes and persuasively argues that
the American poet's cultural role is literally a heroic one.

Holism and Myth in The
Continuity of American Poetry

One thing clearly emerges from Pearce's discussion of the poet's
cultural role. If it is true that the basic style of a historical period can
be the material for mythopoesis, then myth can be a means of viewing
culture holistically through the lens of the poet's myth-making
imagination. The poet finds cultural tension a problem to be solved
because it reflects an imbalance in the inner structures of society. Just
as a geological fault or fracture in the earth results in the exertion of
enormous pressure and cataclysmic surface damage, the tension in the
structure of a culture may exert pressure to cause a serious imbalance in
the functioning of the culture. Poetry, the product of the interaction of
the poet's mind and the culture, aims at a discharge of the tension by
the achievement of a poetic balance at the center of the culture. In this
drama the ubiquitous poet is his own major persona, acting out his role
at the heroic center. Conceived and composed in this epical way, poetry
is an instrumentality for the resolution of cultural problems, the
discharge of cultural tension. What is finally expressed in the poet's
work is the life style of the culture as a whole, made up of the
interacting and interpenetrating basic styles which together constitute
the personality of a people. The style of American culture has been
most clearly reflected in the American epic, but the same problem
pervades all American poetry.

With his method firmly established, Pearce intends in *The Continuity of American Poetry* to exhibit in its historical setting the attempt
that American poets have made to fulfill their traditional cultural role
in the only way which the modern secular world has left them. Pearce
believes that American poets have continuously but unsuccessfully
attempted to resolve cultural tension.

Pearce argues that a pattern runs through all major American poetry.
"The continuity of this narrative is that of the antinomian, Adamic
impulse, as it thrusts against a culture made by Americans who come

more and more to be frightened by it, even as they realize that it is basic to the very idea of their society: one (in Whitman's words) of simple, separate persons, yet democratic, en-masse."[20]

In a seminal article called "The Poet as Person" (1952), Pearce discusses a poetic debate between two modern Americans. He suggests there that the question (of the debate) could be reduced to this: "How could the twentieth-century American tell the truth in poetry? For Williams it was by letting nothing interfere with the poet's need to know himself primarily as an individuated . . . self. For Pound it was by going to school to other poets and learning thereby to delimit and to give precise form to that need – as it were, to put an end to the violence of the self."[21] This debate is a poetic mirror of the tension in values of all American culture; "it is the problem of constructing a society in which men can remain individuals and at the same time share values, ideas, and beliefs, in which they can realize themselves as somehow at once different and alike, separate and together, democratic and en masse."[22] In *The Continuity of American Poetry* Pearce traces this problem from its source in the poetry of the Puritans to its twentieth-century manifestations in Eliot, Pound, Williams, and Stevens.

The deepest and most powerful element of American poetry is what Pearce calls the Adamic impulse. Indeed, in Pearce's view, it is this impulse which marks the course of American poetry as a continuous development. It is this impulse which is the dominating mode of the general style or life style of American culture. This is the impulse toward the violently individuated self as the primary reality.

Its beginning lies in the antinomian reaction against the Puritan's concept of the limits of individual freedom and his idea "that as an individual he could do or make nothing, that all depended on God." The Puritan ideal of a theocratic community, joined together and limited by God's Scriptures, did not raise the problem of the relationship of the individual self to the community. This relationship was carefully defined. Even if only individual men could receive Grace, it was an individuality that became manifested only in men's relationship to God. Thus the Puritans hoped that they had put an end to the history of man's liberation of the self.[23]

But as the Puritan ideal of theocentrism began to waver, antinomianism (or egocentrism) became the dominant force in American
poetry.* As the Puritan culture was pervasive, so its successor,
Romanticism, was pervasive also. Allen Tate believes that the most
important aspect of the Puritan theocracy was the way in which it
permeated every area of life in America, including literature. "It gave
definite meaning to life," says Tate, "the life of pious and impious, of
learned and vulgar alike. It gave – and this is its significance ... an
heroic proportion and a tragic mode to the experience of the
individual."[24] If the Puritan community was made up of individuals
who sensed themselves as individuals only through their sense of God,
then the succeeding "Romantic" community "was made up of
individuals who could acknowledge God only to the degree that their
idea of the godhead demonstrated that they were nothing except as
their individuality made them so." As antinomianism was taken by the
Puritans in the seventeenth century to threaten the very life of the
community, in the Romanticism of the nineteenth century antinomianism was taken to make community possible.[25]

In poetry the change was reflected by a complete transformation of
a theocentric poetry into a poetry of the Adamic mode; from 1830 to
the Civil War was the first great period of American poetry. The force
of the Adamic impulse, however, has remained continuous in American
poetry. Pearce argues that in a sense the history of American poetry is a
history of the Adamic impulse.

In the first great period and in all subsequent periods the problem of
the American poet, both lyric and epic, has remained the same: how to
know himself primarily as an individual and yet to move out of his
egocentricity and effect a resolution between his sense of the violently
individuated self and his sense of the community. Throughout the
history of American poetry this question has been constantly debated.
This debate has sometimes been a public issue, but more often it has
been carried out in the privacy of the poet's own mind as he struggled
alone.

If, as Pearce originally suggested, we conceive of American poetry as

*Pearce uses the terms *egocentrism*, *Adamism*, and *antinomianism* inter-
changeably throughout his discussion.

a series of successive basic styles, then we find that the history of American poetry seems to arrange itself naturally into three periods based on the career of the Adamic impulse: (1) The style or period from 1830 to the Civil War. The most powerful element of this period is the Adamic impulse. (2) The style or period from the Civil War to around 1900. During this period the Adamic impulse becomes exhausted and American poetry becomes sterile. (3) A period from 1900 to the middle of the twentieth century. During this period two styles seem to vie with one another. There is born a "new" poetry by the 1920s which tries an old solution to the tensions of American culture, but Adamism too is revitalized as new possibilities for it are envisioned.

One or two examples from each period will serve to illustrate Pearce's analysis. In the first period the American poet set out to establish a new mode of poetry, a mode of poetry which would create anew himself, his world, and his history. A traditionless land, a disintegrating Puritan theocracy, left him nothing but his own inwardness, his sense of a creative self. In this first great experiment, Pearce argues, the poet tried either to move outward toward the world and universalize his sense of self or to invest the world with his own inwardness by totally internalizing his experience.

Thus Emerson tries to fuse his primary sense of self with his sense of a real world which exists prior to the self. For him, the only way to avoid a sterile solipsism is to impute "his own sensibility to the world in order to understand it as somehow akin to him."[26] This implies that the mind does not take the world as given, but actively engages in a creative ordering of the world. This was Emerson's conception of the task of the poet. But Pearce believes that the poet failed because "for the reader . . . there is no final transmutation of the egocentric into the universal, of man into the world, and vice versa. The egocentrism of Old Adam is there, and we mark it and its limitations as such."[27]

To Whitman, on the other hand, the way into egocentrism is also the way out of it. He intensifies and glories in his ego. He sees that Emerson's precarious balance between the self and the world is out of the question. Instead he refers all experience, belief, thought, and appearance back to the ego, achieving the transformation of the world in terms of his own ego. But as Emerson failed, so too did Whitman. "Discovering and confirming his relationship to the world, the poet discovers the possibility that the nominally anti-poetic can be made into poetry itself. But if he thereby transforms the world, he does not thereby unify it. He gives the world a new meaning – transforming it by alienating it from itself and the crude workaday, anti-poetic reality which characterizes it."[28] But in doing so, he simply ensures his own alienation. He ensures that his own sense of the individual, creating self is intensified.

After the Civil War, American poets, like other Americans, were projected rapidly into the modern world. After 1880 "as the promise of American life appeared uncertain and confused, so did the promise of American poetry."[29] This was a transitional period. The Adamic impulse seemed exhausted as the poet could no longer consider himself an archetypal hero who could re-create a world and its history. His destiny no longer seemed clear.

The pivotal figure of the period in Pearce's analysis is E. A. Robinson, an Adam cast out of the New World, no longer able to transform it but only to name what he witnessed. Robinson's Tilbury Town characters, says Pearce, are men and women in whom egocentrism persists purely as a matter of survival and not as a way of creating and acting, least of all as a way of communicating and making others live. They are men and women in whom egocentrism is carried to its radical conclusion: total solipsism. They live in a village in which all sense of community has vanished. Most of them are resigned to failure or are destroyed by it. On the other hand, they are still meaningful to us as human beings. "For they signify something important in the nature of the modern psyche – even if it is only as they are made to recall, in their inability to communicate directly, a condition and a time when such a thing as self-reliance (in any of its various forms) was a radical possibility for all men. In them, Robinson pushes to an outer limit a sense of the exhaustion, perhaps the bankruptcy, of the simple, separate person."[30] The exhaustion of an entire cultural style is reflected in the radical isolation of Robinson's characters. By 1920 the depleted Adamic mode was succeeded by a new kind of American poetry in a new mode.

The "new" mode is actually a very old one. Pearce calls it the "mythic" mode.* The mythic mode depends upon a transcendent power for its authority and on tradition for its world. The mythic mode in America has taken two forms: a poetry which seeks its roots in the European (and more specifically the Anglo-Saxon) tradition and a poetry which is largely regional but which also depends on religious orthodoxy. The poets who have used the mythic mode include some of America's greatest. Pearce traces the line of mythic poets from Pound and Eliot through the Fugitives, chiefly Ransom and Tate. With these poets, "the mythic poem took its most appropriate shape, as it leaned toward regionalism, tradition, orthodox religion, and an overpowering sense of the past — all principles of continuity derived from those large, extra-human, form-giving patterns of belief and commitment called myths."[31]

But the mythic mode is necessarily doomed as a viable form for American poets. Just as the exhaustion of the Adamic impulse seems to have called forth its opposite, the mythic poem, this in its turn called forth a revival of the Adamic poem. As the countercurrent of the mythic poetry began to be felt, the current of the continuity of American poetry began to revive.[32] Pearce seems almost to suggest that the life style of the culture itself responded as though to a general attack. At any rate, the twentieth-century issue of American poetry had been joined and is as yet not completely settled.

It is now possible, perhaps, to draw some specific conclusions about Pearce's position with regard to myth and American culture. Surely *The Continuity of American Poetry* fulfills Pearce's earlier request for "some integrated, genuinely holistic view" of culture in which "the form of the discipline reflects the sense of the wholeness of the civilization."[33]

The form of the study of American culture should, according to Pearce's view, be integrated so that the interpenetrating basic styles of all the various aspects of the culture yield a comprehensive view of the general style of the culture. Each individual researcher contributes to

*It is sometimes difficult to follow Pearce in this part of his discussion. For example, he has already implied the mythic mode was not viable for American poets. Yet at this stage of his discussion he seems to have changed his mind.

the total understanding of the general style of the culture through a thorough study of the basic style of his own interest. The study of poetry is, of course, fundamental because of the poet's privileged position. Thus Pearce's work is an "inside narrative." By utilizing insights from psychology and anthropology, Pearce tries to lay the foundation for a total understanding of the general or life style of American culture in *The Continuity of American Poetry*: the book views culture as a whole; it insists that culture has a functioning organic structure, exhibited by the very existence of a general or life style; it suggests that culture has thematic continuity as reflected in the fact that the character or style has a temporal aspect and may be treated historically; and it posits an impersonal agency (the Adamic impulse) as a dynamic force in culture.

Pearce's theoretical orientation, derived from cultural anthropology and holism, places him squarely with writers like MacIver, Kimball Young, and Bronislaw Malinowski. Myth is culturally spawned; it is the instrument for adjustment to the social-cultural environment. American poets, necessarily writing from within the limitation of the basic style of their idiom, attempt to solve their own (and consequently everyone's) problem of relating to culture. By transcending cultural polarity poetically, with himself at the center, the poet creates a mythic-heroic balance and discharges cultural tensions. Such a view implies a holistic conception of myth, for myths are understandable only as they are related to the dominant concerns of a specific (and whole) culture. In a like manner it implies that an intimate knowledge of a culture is accessible only through its life style as it is reflected in the culture's dominant myths. A complex and highly developed viewpoint, Pearce's theory raises several perplexing questions.

Problems and Accomplishments

Pearce's analysis of American culture raises a general problem, which for the sake of simplicity we may call *cultural isolationism*. If we assume (as holism seems to force us to do) that myths are caused by specific and unique cultural conditions, then we must conclude that the myths of one culture are totally distinct and isolated from the myths of other cultures, especially, it seems, if they are separated by a great distance temporally.*

Yet how can this view of myth be reconciled with studies in comparative culture? All cultures have produced hero myths. Both the form (a heroic figure) and the theme (the salvation of a culture) have crossed cultural boundaries throughout history. An extreme holism which sees all causal factors solely in the cultural environment cannot account for this historical fact. It seems just as reasonable (and perhaps more urgent) to ask for the meaning of the hero myth for the entire race of man as to insist, as does holism, on the cultural insularity of the causes and conditions of the development of the hero myth.

Furthermore, Pearce does not establish that the mythification process carried out by the American poet is unique. Indeed, the process seems to be the poetic analogue to a primitive ritual in which, historians of religion tell us, man invests his world with the sacred before he attempts to establish his abode there. Mircea Eliade describes this ritual as an attempt to eliminate chaos. In primitive cultures, it has been found, men perform a ritual which symbolically duplicates the work of a transcendent power, a ritual which constructs the cosmos and creates the world anew.[34] The essential step in constructing a sacred reality in space is the establishment of the *axis mundi*, the cosmic axis or center of the world. The importance of the *axis mundi* is that it renders order from chaos by establishing communication between earth, heaven, and the underworld. For the archaic man, the habitable world extends from this center. A universe comes to birth from its center, precisely where space becomes sacred. This "creation of the world becomes the archetype of every human gesture, whatever the plane of reference may be."[35] The sacred abode is an organic metaphor for the cosmos.

A "completely profane world, the wholly desacralized cosmos, is a recent discovery," Eliade contends.[36] In archaic societies men lived as much as possible in the sacred. This was possible because, for primitive

*I am aware of the criticism which might be raised here that I am unfair to Pearce since nowhere does he make such a statement nor would he agree with it. My main concern, however, is to examine the implications of his holistic assumptions which lead to conclusions that, if carefully examined, he might wish to reject. As we will see, each of the other authors makes similar assumptions which result in conclusions that, I believe, they might also reject.

man, the sacred manifests itself as something which is wholly different from the profane and the whole of nature is capable of revealing itself as sacred. On the other hand, Eliade comments, for modern man "desacralization pervades his entire experience," and "he finds it increasingly difficult to rediscover the existential dimensions of religious man in the archaic societies."[37]

In like manner, Pearce describes the American poet's discovery of a desacralized world with no transcendent authority, no "source in some *numen*, some absolutely authoritative power." If the *numinous*, the holy, the absolute other is absent from the modern world, how can the world become a sacred epiphany? There is no transcendent power which would make viable "that culture hero required to make a proper epic." The American poet, in trying to write an epic when the transcendent source for the epic is no longer to be found, turns to himself. "In what could the poet believe," queries Pearce, "except in his power to believe? In whom could he believe except himself?"[38] Turning from a transcendent power, the American poet has concentrated upon an epiphany of self at the center of his culture. He has envisioned "a time and a condition of the imaginative use of language when mythification, or something like it, would be altogether possible. The history of the American epic," says Pearce, "is the history of attempts to realize that possibility."[39] This "possibility," if realized, would infuse the poet's (and man's) world with the sacred. The poet himself would function as the *axis mundi*, the center of the world.

Pearce's description of the quest of the American poet for the means of writing a new epic which will serve its traditional cultural purpose bears a striking similarity to Eliade's description of archaic man's quest to found his abode in the sacred. The change from the suprahuman level to the human level was necessitated by the progressive and historical desacralization of the cosmos. The point is, however, that the ritual aspects of both exhibit such a startling similarity, a similarity that suggests man's need to live in a sacred cosmos. This cosmos, so easily available to primitive man, and denied to modern man, is ritually supplied by the poet's desperate "drenching of reality."* Surely

---

*"Drenching of reality" is a phrase used by Henry Thoreau in *Walden* to designate the same process that Pearce describes of transmuting the total environment.

American culture *is* unique and yet is *not* isolated. The American poet's solution to an old problem is unique, but the problem itself has crossed countless cultural boundaries.

Whitman's work stands as a model of a culturally unique response to an ageless longing. In *Song of Myself* the poet is at the center of a rich profusion of creativity. The world flows from him as its primal source. He is the guarantor of himself, his world, and his history. In Whitman's ceaseless inventories, the world comes into being as the poet names its inhabitants. The poet is the organic metaphor of the world and at the same time he performs the very act of creation.[40] Is this not what Eliade describes as reproducing "the work of the gods," creating "the world anew"? To Whitman, the world has no natural order, no structure; it is chaos. But it is this world to which he and all men must relate, because it is a brute fact of their existence in which they must discover (or create) themselves. Pearce writes: "What is relatively stable and fixed ... is the world of which that [the poet's] sensibility ... discovers itself. The world is too large, too much, to have an imitable order or pattern. It is just there. The hero's hope in *Song of Myself*, his ... object, is to know that the world is there, and in the knowing, to know that *he* is there. In effect, through such a transaction he would create himself, only then to 'find' himself. ..."[41] Once the poet has defined his relation to the world, he is in a position to control it or to create it anew for all men. "He no longer needs to seek his world ... he can openly and lovingly address it, as he at once creates and controls it and as he is created and controlled by it. He is thus a religion, God-like in himself: 'I am an acme of things accomplish'd, and I am encloser of things to be.' "[42] As he confronts the world in this dynamic process, "the hero releases the full creative force of the self, defines the *realia* of his world and takes from them his name, his office, and his phenomenal, existential qualities. He fathers, delivers, and baptizes himself."[43] Thus, he reinvests the world with the sacred as he founds his abode in it. He has, as Eliade says, established "a fixed and sacred center." This poetic act, this "creation of the world," is "the archetype of every human gesture."[44]

In the light of Eliade's discussion, it appears that the American poet in the modern world is fulfilling an ancient, even primordial ritual. The archetypal gesture, rather than being part of a native American myth holistically spawned and culturally isolated, is actually transcultural and is the survival of archaic ritual myth. This aspect of myth, this approach to myth, should not be ignored. Yet those who follow the holistic school of modern cultural anthropology tend to ignore this approach, if not to dismiss it. This is in part due to an overcommitment to the belief that a culture is a unique entity and hence that it generates its own unique myths.

Pearce's discussion raises another question which I believe must be resolved by Pearce or others if the concept of cultural style is to fulfill its promise as a methodological tool. The problem centers specifically in Pearce's concept of Adamism, which early in the text he identifies with an antinomian, egocentric impulse originating in the Calvinist culture of the seventeenth century: "The continuity of this narrative is that of the antinomian, Adamic impulse, as it thrusts against a culture made by Americans who come more and more to be frightened by it. . . ."[45] Again and again the word *impulse* appears to describe the continuity among the poets Pearce discusses. Later he substitutes the word *mode* for *impulse* more and more often. Harmless if the two words were equivalent, the change actually has grave implications in Pearce's discussion. The two words themselves are the key to the difference. *Mode* suggests a manner, a method, or a particular form — something which is in itself an abstraction and therefore static; *impulse* suggests the act of impelling, or driving onward with force. The difference between these words is not simply one of degree.

Pearce identifies the Adamic *mode* as the basic style of American poetry. As we noted, he defines basic style as a "mode and strategy," a "pattern and plan-of-attack . . . a necessary condition of artistic creation." "It never exists as such in a poem, or even in a poet's whole work. Rather, it is immanent there. . . . And the historian, knowing that it exists in a pure state only in his mind, as a historical construct, must try to make it explicit. . . . He must always work back toward the basic style from the unique styles of the poems. . . ."[46] Adamism as a style is a conceptual heuristic model, an ideal type to be filled in and made explicit. "The Adamic poem — to define it as a basic style, a kind of ideal type — is one which . . . forms and is formed by the vision of the world in which it has being."[47]

Max Weber, in his account of the construction and use of ideal types by the social sciences, states that these constructs are "arrived at by the . . . accentuation of certain elements of reality." "In its conceptual purity, this mental construct . . . cannot be found empirically anywhere in reality. . . . Historical research faces the task of determining in each individual case, the extent to which [the] ideal-construct approximates to or diverges from reality."[48] In its pure form the ideal type cannot be found in reality because it is constructed by stressing and abstracting certain empirical aspects of reality. Once conceived, however, the mental construct is an indispensable "heuristic and expository" device in the social sciences. The usefulness of the ideal type is established by historical research to fill out the details of the construct.

But, as we have seen, one of the characteristics of holism is to suggest that in an organic functioning cultural whole, the dynamic process is extrapersonal. Historical or social change is not viewed as a consequence of human agency. Indeed, human beings are impelled by the process. Their thoughts, their attitudes, their feelings are formed by cultural forces over which they have little or no control. To a holist, the ideal type as a heuristic construct is not enough. He must, by the logic of his position, reify the construct and view it as a causal force in its own sphere.

The mode, Adamism, is either an abstract concept or a reality. Obviously the holist cannot have it both ways. No matter how useful the construct is for understanding certain cultural phenomena, there is no evidence to support a conclusion that the abstraction exists as an independent causal force or impulse. A mode, a form, does not impel. The suggestion of causality attached to "impulse" raises a problem which Pearce does not resolve. If Adamism has causal efficacy, he must show that it does. To simply call Adamism an impulse is to beg the question unless he can show specifically how it impels.

On the other hand, if we construe Adamism as a mode or pattern, the problem of causality is irrelevant since an ideal type does not purport to explain phenomena but only to exhibit similarity or continuity. The problem remains, however, of validating Pearce's theory by filling in the details of the construct by historical research. This is the most difficult of all the tasks Pearce faced in writing his complex book. He is not entirely successful.

Pearce's problem perhaps arises from the inflexibility of a theory which hopes to explain *all* phenomena of a particular class. In other words, the theory purports to show that the work of all major American poets can be explained by Adamism. Karl Popper has suggested that the difference between knowledge and pseudoknowledge lies in the possibility of refutation; if a theory may possibly be disproved, it may also be verifiable, but a theory that seems to explain everything, such as Freudian psychology or Marxian historicism, can never be refuted. It is a faith and must be accepted or rejected on other than scientific grounds.

Here we must ask the holistic theorist how we may go about refuting his theory, at least in principle. But Pearce's theory insists that the work of *all* American poets of note is the product of a dominant or basic style of culture. When he encounters a major practical difficulty, such as the divergence of an important poet from the theoretical construct, he accounts for the divergence in terms of his theory.

Two results of theoretical inflexibility are illustrated in Pearce's treatment of E. A. Robinson. Robinson, who does not seem to fit the model, is made to conform, and as a consequence his poetry receives undue critical attention. Pearce argues that Robinson's work is an aesthetic failure. But he insists that Robinson is a pivotal figure because in him the Adamic impulse is exhausted.[49] If we translate this, does it not simply mean that Robinson's work bears little resemblance to the model we have been using?

Yet by stressing Robinson's work as pivotal, Pearce seems to conclude that the poet's work has great merit *because* it is an artistic failure. Indeed, he strongly suggests that Robinson is at his best when he is failing. But this is a paradoxical way of being at one's best. The paradox almost certainly results from the elevation of Adamism to a criterion of literary merit. By reflecting the exhaustion of the Adamic impulse (i.e., not fitting the model), Robinson's work is judged in terms of Adamism and perforce Robinson becomes a "great" American poet.

Adamism is surely an odd aesthetic category. A reasonable critical evaluation of the mean and the great in poetry must be based on a careful consideration of the body of the poet's work. A conclusion about the success or failure of individual poems must be based on the evaluation of those specific poems. If E. A. Robinson or any other poet is not of the first rank, it is perhaps because he lacks a crucial talent, fails to use language adequately, creates vague images, has no lyric quality, lacks dramatic power, or exhibits any one of many possible faults. But surely a poet is neither great nor small because of his relationship to the Adamic impulse.

III

America's Cultural Home: Smith's *Virgin Land*

The Conceptual Framework: The Unity of Imagination, Thought, and Action

Virgin Land (1950) is a pioneering effort to treat imaginative literature concurrently with political and economic ideas as a part of the broad sweep of cultural history, while at the same time recognizing the essential differences between the two kinds of material. Its impact is still difficult to assess. Smith's greatest influence is the stimulation that he has given to the infant discipline of American Studies and to scholars venturing into new and strange paths of research. *Virgin Land* was the first book dealing with large aspects of American culture in terms of myth and symbol, but since its appearance there has been a steady stream of similar publications, of which *The Continuity of American Poetry, Andrew Jackson, Symbol for an Age*, and *The American Adam* are only three significant examples. Whether or not another author follows Smith precisely, anyone beginning the study of American intellectual and social history must take his work into account.

The main task the author sets for himself in *Virgin Land* is to study the extraordinary response of the American people during the nineteenth century to the unknown, vast, and virtually empty land west of the eastern mountain chain. The response was on two levels: thought and action. *Virgin Land* is, then, in one sense, concerned with the interrelationship between thought and action in American culture. But since human thought and action involve human values, the relationship among thought, action, and value is also one of the subjects of *Virgin Land*. On the level of thought, Smith is concerned with imaginative literature and all social, political, and economic theory that goes beyond the purely logical or empirical level to the imaginative level of ideas. On the level of action, he aims at comprehending the physical human response provoked by the rich imaginative conception of the American West. It is, perhaps, at the level of human values that the great significance of Smith's work lies, for, like Pearce, Smith moves toward the goal of an integrated vision of culture in which human value must be inevitably and tightly interwoven into the texture of cultural thought and action.

For his themes, Smith takes the historical careers of three imaginative conceptions connected with the West: the rugged men of the frontier called "sons of Leatherstocking," the "passage to India," and the "garden of the world." Closely connected to the garden is the "yeoman" farmer. Smith defines myth and symbol as "larger or smaller units of the same kind of thing."[1] This implies that the difference between them is only one of degree and that myth and symbol are not different kinds of things. We will find that the passage to India and the garden of the world are myths and the yeoman farmer is a symbol. It is more difficult to decide about the figure of the frontiersman, but it is clear that Smith intends that he be treated as a symbol — though perhaps a symbol in a larger myth.

Although the treatment of mythical and symbolic elements of the human imagination poses a problem in methodology, Smith, unlike Pearce, has not attempted to develop a systematic theory of culture. Yet an implicit theory underlies his specific treatment of the myths of the West in *Virgin Land*. Beyond the book itself there is a source that helps us to understand his procedure, the article "Can 'American Studies' Develop a Method?"

The problem of method in American Studies, Smith declares, arises only because a study of American culture "as a whole does not coincide with the customary field of operations of any established academic discipline."[2] The thrust of Smith's article is that American Studies should attempt to develop a methodology which can treat large or whole aspects of American culture across the arbitrary lines laid down by the established disciplines.

Again and again Smith implies that value occupies the center of the cultural stage and that the difficulty of treating values is the most important single methodological problem: "The concept 'culture' seems, in the abstract at least, to embrace the concepts 'society' and 'art.' Why may we not say quite simply that the problem of method in American Studies can be solved by presupposing a value implicit in culture which includes and reconciles the apparently disparate values assumed in the disciplines of, say, literature and sociology."[3] Terms like *reconciles* and *disparate values* suggest that Smith sees the central task of methodology as the restoration of the study of cultural values to its rightful place.

Smith clarifies this further when he discusses the shortcomings of the present methods of comprehending cultural values, shortcomings which have made it impossible to deal with values in the sociocultural sciences. The New Critics, for example, in spite of their contributions, have been an obstacle: Eliot's definition of literature as a timeless order of eternal objects had the effect of moving literature outside time and accordingly made it "unhistorical or even antihistorical."[4] It consequently became extremely difficult to relate literature to its historical or cultural context.

The empirical bias of the social sciences has been just as great a deterrent to the study of culture in America. Where "the literary critic would cut aesthetic value loose from social fact . . . the social scientist . . . uses techniques of research which make it difficult or impossible for him to deal with the states of consciousness embodied in serious art."[5] Phenomena which are not susceptible of statistical analysis are useless to social scientists. At best, social scientists can only analyze the content of large quantities of popular fiction or drama or humor. But content analyses cannot be adapted to the works of art which we consider great because great works of art are precisely those which are also unique. What we need is "a method that can give us access to meanings beyond the range of such a systematic simplification — meanings that are not, so to speak, homogenized. Lacking such a method, the sociological study of the arts will inevitably yield an image of the culture which is truncated."[6]

Smith turns to his own study of Mark Twain for examples of the kinds of problems a scholar has that are holistic in nature. One of these is the problem of Mark Twain's style. Much like Pearce, Smith sees that style is an important cultural index. He views it chiefly as an indicator of an author's attitudes toward the culture with which he is interacting and the values in it he esteems. These values reflect the structure of the culture and are formed before an author writes his books. To speak of the autonomy of a work of art in such a case is ridiculous. The autonomy of a novel was impaired "by forces that were in large part internalized by the author" long before he sat down to write. Twain's style has two sources, and it is Smith's contention that we can neglect neither. If we neglect to examine Twain's craftsmanship and the purely artistic and aesthetic aspect of his writing, we have failed in our task of comprehending Twain. If we neglect to examine the culture in which his work flowered — its assumptions and values — then we have also failed to comprehend Twain. These tasks cannot be separated because Twain's artistic development took place in a cultural context. But the attitudes that spring from conscious reflection need to be distinguished from those taken over unconsciously from the culture.[7]

Since the problems Twain faced as an author, which shaped his literary development, were determined by the culture in which he lived in the late nineteenth century, they cannot be dealt with by literary methods alone. "Many of the forces at work in the fiction are clearly of social origin." The kind of method that is needed is one both literary and sociological — a holistic method which would reveal new insights into American culture. Such insights are possible, according to Smith, because Twain's problems, attitudes, and characteristics were not peculiar to him. "They were widely current in American literature and thought; they are cultural, not merely private and individual, images."[8]

These cultural and social forces that shape the thought of such men as Mark Twain are Smith's chief concern in *Virgin Land*. Since the image of the West became one of the great controlling forces in nineteenth-century American thought and imagination, and more importantly played a large part in conditioning social and political action, it must be understood if we are to comprehend why men responded to it as they did. The reciprocal influence of imagination, thought, and action makes works of the imagination major repositories of unconscious cultural values and attitudes which propel men to act.

The relationship that Smith suggests inheres between cultural forces and style, the way that attitudes and values are internalized and cultural problems shape artistic development, are all characteristic of what has been defined here as a holistic view of culture. The cultural or social unit in Smith's conceptual framework is clearly more than the mere sum of its members, for it must be treated only, he declares, as a whole. His insistence that style, artistic values, moral values, and class attitudes cannot be separated without distortion emphasizes his holistic commitment.

Smith's Use of Myth: Myth, Fact, and Value

Smith has called for a method that will not atomize and hence distort culture but will comprehend organic complexes as they actually exist in the culture. He has implicitly suggested that the products of human thought and imagination might be the richest and deepest sources of material in which a scholar can begin his research. Because they are mutual creations, and not private and individual, myths are the highest embodiments of human imagination.*

In a brief preface to *Virgin Land* Smith defines his two central concepts: myth and symbol.† Myth and symbol are "larger or smaller units of the same kind of thing, namely an intellectual construction that fuses concept and emotion into an image. The myths and symbols with which I deal have the further characteristic of being collective representations rather than the work of a single mind."[9] Several key ideas in the definition need clarification in order to show their

---

*Smith does not exclude the possibility of private myths, but he has no concern for them in *Virgin Land*.

† *Virgin Land* has recently been reissued by Harvard University Press (1970) with a new preface. The major change Smith makes is to suggest that the relationship between myth and empirical fact is more complicated than he himself originally suggested in 1950. His comment simply supports my analysis. But the central question remains to be answered: what is the relationship of myth and symbol to empirical fact?

relationship to each other: image; myths and symbols; the fusion of concept and emotion; collective representations. By image, Smith seems to mean a concrete, but collective, representation which has a core idea or set in interrelated ideas having historical continuity and exercising a degree of control on thought and imagination. Images then are often improvisations on a single idea or concept. The frontiersman, personified by Daniel Boone in fact and legend and by Leatherstocking in literature, was an ambivalent concept to the American imagination. To some, the frontiersman was an image of a fugitive from civilization, an anarchical figure fleeing ever westward in front of an advancing line of settlements. To others, he was a trailblazer for the farmers who followed him and an empire builder on the side of civilization and American destiny.[10] As a trailblazer, the frontiersman helped to open up a continent and prepared the way for what was to become the dominant nineteenth-century concept of the West as the garden of the world. The core idea of the frontiersman contained the potential of two similar but still radically different images having totally different symbolic import: an anarchical figure and a trailblazer for civilization.

There is a second, even more important example of the way in which a core idea can project radically different images. Smith time and again identifies the American West as producing one of the unifying ideas of nineteenth-century American culture. He points out the enormous impact of the great empty land mass west of the Alleghenies. Its effect was vague but present even before the beginning of the nineteenth century. "At the opening of the eighteenth century the image of the West beyond the Appalachian Mountains was very dim in the minds of those subjects of the British crown who inhabited the fringe of colonies along the Atlantic coast."[11] British economic policy kept this image from developing along any definite lines throughout almost the entire eighteenth century, "but the American West was nevertheless there, a physical fact of great if unknown magnitude. It strongly influenced the debate over the nature of the [British] Empire which preceded the Revolution."[12] By the end of the American Revolution the concept of the West had begun to achieve definite outlines. Quoting from a piece by Philip Freneau written in 1782, Smith points out that "the physical fact of the continent dominates the scene" which Freneau describes.[13]

But a more important fact in Freneau's and others' early concepts of the American West is that they embody two different, if often mingled, images. One image is that of the West as essentially a great highway which would become the connecting link for trade between Europe and India. This was a conception based on the notion of America as a great commercial maritime empire dominating the sea. The second image is that of the development of the West into an internal and continental agrarian utopia. The importance of these two images is that they furnish the material for two of the great myths about the American West: the passage to India and the garden of the world.

Smith's account suggests that the core idea behind the myths, the idea of the American West, has a life of its own and a continuity which is identifiable whatever image of it the myth projects. The idea of the American West is identified by Smith as "one of the most persistent generalizations concerning American life and character." It is "the notion that our society has been shaped by the pull of a vacant continent drawing population westward through the passes of the Alleghenies, across the Mississippi Valley, over the high plains and mountains of the Far West to the Pacific Coast."[14] Several myths and symbols have gathered around this conception and characterized it. This central idea in effect reflects the unalterable unity of culture as a whole, which unity shows itself through those myths and symbols that characterize the idea. The myths may support different and even conflicting images of the West, but the core idea is always the same – in this instance, the American West.

This reflection of cultural unity is possible because of the fusion of concept and emotion that occurs as myth and symbol take form. The fusion of concept and emotion into myth is precisely the reason why Smith earlier called for a holistic approach to cultural values, for this fusion of concept and emotion into myth and symbol results in an imaginative creation going beyond the conceptual level. Smith again and again identifies the imaginative mythic creations with the matrix of cultural values. The myth that came to dominate the nineteenth century was the garden of the world. It was "a collective representation, a poetic idea . . . that defined the promise of American life. The master symbol of the garden embraced a cluster of metaphors expressing fecundity, growth, increase, and blissful labor in the earth, all centering about the heroic figure of the idealized frontier farmer armed with that supreme agrarian weapon, the sacred plow."[15] The major cultural role of myth is to express "the assumptions and aspirations of a whole society."[16] Once we have identified the dominant myths of a culture, it follows that we can isolate and comprehend with fresh insight the fundamental values that control and motivate the culture.

Myths objectify cultural values, ideals, and even goals. Things usually treated separately — concept and emotion, fact and value, logic and imagination — are in fact reconciled on the cultural level. In his article Smith only suggests why a holistic approach to cultural behavior is *useful.* In *Virgin Land* he shows why a holistic approach is *required.* Myths and symbols are cultural creations, what Smith calls "collective representations." They are created and believed by a large number of people within a culture and have specific historical continuity. Since they express the most sacred values and aspirations of the society and reflect the inner spirit of the society, it is reasonable to assume that by studying such myths it is possible to learn a great deal about the society from the "inside," in Pearce's phrase.

One of the most important reasons for studying myth lies in its ability to influence cultural behavior. In his preface Smith declares that he does not intend to raise the question of whether or not myth corresponds to an empirical state of affairs because myths "exist on a different plane. But . . . they sometimes exert a decided influence on practical affairs."[17] For example, the dominant myth — the garden of the world — shaped the image of the American West as an agricultural paradise, "embodying group memories of an earlier, a simpler and, it was believed, a happier state of society, [which] long survived as a force in American thought and politics." Indeed, the image was so powerful "down to the very end of the nineteenth century [that] it continued to seem a representation . . . of the core of the nation."[18] One of Smith's examples of the power of this myth is in politics. The myth of the garden, argues Smith, was implicit even in the early notion of a passage to India over a great continental empire. But before an empire could develop, there would be a long period during which the

West would be developed. The development would naturally be agricultural. This assumption emerged on the level of rational and imaginative interpretation as an agrarian social theory. The theory insisted that agriculture was the only real source of wealth and demanded free land for all in the West. The concrete imaginative focus for the theory was the symbol of the yeoman — the idealized farmer. Agricultural utopianism and the idealized farmer remained crucial forces in political decisions, campaigns, economic programs, and indeed elections throughout the nineteenth century. They remain to a lesser degree powerful even today.[19]

Theoretically, myths clearly have great methodological importance. They furnish fresh insights into a culture, and they influence the same culture they reflect. They are the creation of powerful cultural forces growing out of the deepest dreams, desires, and aspirations of the people. In myth the facts of physical nature, history, economics, and politics are united with human nature, emotion, and imagination. On the cultural-mythic level, fact and value are merged and must be studied as a unit, for it is only as a unit that fact and value have meaning. This is the reason Smith insists that either a purely literary approach or a purely sociological approach to cultural phenomena will inevitably fail to comprehend the meaning of the phenomena as they are related to the whole culture.

Holism and Myth in Virgin Land

It is now possible to see specific relationships among culture, myth, value, and action. An unavoidable question arises: What are the causes of myths? That is, what are the forces that bring about the growth of myth from the culture? Why does one myth dominate others which have roots in and grow from the same culture? This is not a psychological question (at least not in *Virgin Land*), but a cultural question. In other words, what are the cultural conditions out of which myths grow; what are the forces that produce these "collective representations" which have such powerful and controlling influence on our lives?

The simplest answer that can be given to the question is *need*. In *Virgin Land* myths tend to follow the lines laid down by social, economic, and sometimes political need. An enlightening illustration of this point is Smith's discussion of the relationship between the myth of the garden and the myth of the American desert. As the advancing frontier moved further west and gradually edged out onto the arid desert country of the Great Plains, the settlers encountered two forces which were against them: climatic conditions and (even more formidable) a myth directly opposed to the garden of the world – the myth of the desert. The advance surged onto the arid plains spurred on by the simple physical existence of the western land mass offering economic and social opportunity to great numbers of dispossessed and disillusioned people and also by the image of the West as a garden – a great pastoral utopia. But the sheer physical hardship of the desert was brutal. "On the level of the imagination it was therefore necessary that the settler's battle with drought and dust and wind and grasshoppers should be supported by the westward extension of the myth of the garden. In order to establish itself in the vast new area of the plains, however, the myth of the garden had to confront and overcome another myth of exactly opposed meaning, although of inferior strength – the myth of the Great American Desert."[20] The image of the Great Plains supported by the desert myth, Smith explains, had prevailed since the early nineteenth century. If anything, this concept exaggerated the aridity and physical hardships of the desert country. In imaginative literature it was conceived as an area friendly only to "hostile brigands" and a menace to agricultural areas and people. Obviously such a myth ran counter to the driving economic and social need for settlers to penetrate the area and continue westward. One of the conflicting myths had to give way. "As settlement moved up the valleys of the Platte and the Kansas rivers," comments Smith, "the myth of the desert was destroyed and in its stead the myth of the garden of the world was projected out across the plains."[21]

The destruction of the desert myth began with the idea that somehow providentially as the settlers began to move onto the plains, rainfall mysteriously increased. Ultimately, when the desert myth had been completely replaced by the myth of the garden, writers refused even to "admit that the interior basin beyond the Rockies is a desert" at all and concluded that "the trans-Mississippi as a whole . . . 'is destined to be the garden of the world.' "[22] Clearly sheer human *need* plays an enormous and perhaps decisive part in the dynamics of myth production. Myth production becomes instrumental in the success and fulfillment of human necessity. As we will see, this places Smith solidly in the camp of MacIver and Kimball Young.

At this point, it is possible to draw some conclusions about Smith's conception of the nature of myth and to compare and contrast his conception with the models discussed in chapter I. Myth is connected to culture holistically because it fuses fact, need, and value into one imaginative whole which reflects the dominant aspirations and assumptions of the entire culture. The more homogeneous the result of this fusion is, the stronger, the more efficacious, and the longer lasting the myth will be. It may conflict with other, similar myths and its strength will be tested as were the strengths of the garden of the world and the American desert myths in their conflicts.

Myths have great causal efficacy. Large segments of the population will conceive of reality precisely in terms of myths. They are structurally identical with MacIver's "dominant thought forms" in that they are ideological, valuational responses which tend instrumentally to support social and cultural growth in a specific direction. To MacIver, myths are the sustaining instruments for the achievement of cultural and social as well as economic ends. To Smith, valuational thought is imaginative and is therefore best expressed in myth. Myths are the imaginative fusion of needs and values which are instrumental for action and sustain long-range cultural aims — as in the example of the myth of the garden which overcomes the desert myth.

In the cultural matrix the relationship among nature (level of fact), need, value, and action forms a causal nexus which can be diagrammatically illustrated; see figure 1. Smith's conceptual framework suggests (to paraphrase a remark once made by John Dewey) that values arise where a lack is perceived to exist. Myths follow needs and values and are instrumental to action. They also sustain action over long periods of time, as the conception of the West embodied implicit assumptions about the proper nature of society and was a constant goad to action. This characteristic of myth, in fact, produces one of the key problems of cultural crises since myths tend to become self-sustaining entities

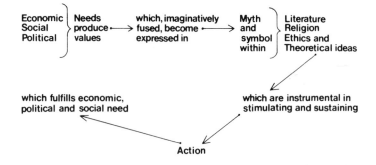

Figure 1. The cultural matrix

having a profound controlling impact on human events. Like one of MacIver's dominant thought forms, a myth is internalized and becomes a basic mode of perceiving reality. Perpetuated in this way, a myth may outlast its usefulness as the instrumental support for needful action. The original need may disappear many years, even decades, before the myth begins to be questioned. In some instances, a myth may become a deterrent to required action when new needs and values begin to emerge under changing conditions.

This is, in effect, what happened to the myth of the garden of the world. According to Smith, as myths "lose their pertinence to a changed social setting, they often become bad influences by lending themselves to the uses of men who wish merely to confuse issues. The myth of the garden suffered this fate."[2 3] By the 1870s it had already been invoked to avoid land reform. The myth of the garden assumed an almost unlimited supply of fertile land as the basis of its vision of paradise. But not only was there no such unlimited quantity of land; much of the existent land was not profitably arable because of the scarcity of rainfall. Realizing what this could mean in terms of human suffering and defeat, some reformers fought to increase the acreage allowed to each settler under the Homestead Act. They also fought to reform the corrupt Land Office itself. When a deciding struggle actually came in Congress in the winter of 1878-1879, the reformers lost. Smith argues that the most telling cause of their defeat was that their proposals seemed to violate the myth of the garden. "The enlarged homestead grants proposed for the arid plains would destroy the time-honored ideal of a society of yeoman subsistence farmers."[24] The opponents of the reform insisted that an increase in the amount of free land for each settler would create great estates and spawn an aristocracy. The true reasons for the collapse of the Homestead system were again and again veiled by the mythic elements which held men's minds. The reformers were in essence asking for a revision of one of the central tenets of the myth to make it accord with the changing facts of human need. But the "demand was too stringent; the myth could not be transformed so easily."[25] The revision would have to wait for a later day.

Smith's theoretical orientation is, like Pearce's, derived largely from cultural anthropology and holism. A specific myth is produced by a specific culture. No other culture could have produced precisely the same myth as the garden of the world, for no other culture could conceivably have the same problems and needs. A myth is unique just as a culture is unique. Myth is, in addition, the instrument for achieving cultural ends and solving problems of adjustment and need. This places Smith, again like Pearce, solidly with writers such as MacIver, Kimball Young, and Bronislaw Malinowski, all of whom agree that culture is a self-generative, self-perpetuating, and dynamic whole. In other words, it is the complex matrix of the systems of concepts and usages, organizations, and instruments by means of which men in a culture deal with physical, biological, and human nature in the satisfaction of their needs.

Accomplishments and Problems

Virgin Land illustrates that it is impossible to discuss mythopoesis and culture without developing a theory of myth and its relationship to culture. Smith begins with an ostensibly vague conceptual framework but one which is implicit and highly developed in the work itself. The conditions out of which myths grow are various needs, although economic need seems to be the most important stimulus for myth. Need produces values, which are crystallized in myths. Myths in turn stimulate the action which is necessary to fulfill need. In his article

"Can 'American Studies' Develop a Method?" Smith calls for a holistic method which will help to heal the division between the quantitative and the qualitative study of culture. Smith's theory of myth moves determinedly in that direction, for, according to his theory, cultural facts and cultural values become fused in myth. Properly understood, his theory should give historians and critics new insight into cultural processes.

One of the most important consequences of Smith's work in *Virgin Land* is a method of analyzing cultural values according to their function. As we saw, some myths and some values may outlast their instrumental function. This may simply be a fact of human psychology and consequently inevitable. Nevertheless, it is a possibility of which the cultural historian must be aware.

Smith's use of his method to investigate cultural values opens up the startling possibility that in the social sciences myth infuses hypotheses that ostensibly rest on solid empirical documentation. The most effective use of this insight is Smith's explanation of the appeal of Frederick Jackson Turner's thesis to American historians. Turner's famous hypothesis was that American democratic institutions are unique to the American continent rather than continuous with European institutions. It insisted that the availability of free land on the frontier explained the particular pattern of the development of American social and political institutions. This broad thesis attained an enormous vogue among "a whole generation of historians" who set out to rewrite "American history in terms of it."[26]

But Smith's aim is to show that "brilliant and persuasive" as it was, Turner's "contention that the frontier and the West had dominated American development could hardly have attained such universal acceptance if it had not found an echo in ideas and attitudes already current."[27] In other words, the very acceptability of Turner's thesis was not due so much to its intrinsic ability to explain the existence of a special form of American institutions as to the fact that the American consciousness had already been conditioned to embrace such a thesis. This conditioning was the result of an entire century of "persistent generalizations" claiming an inexhaustible efficacy for the power of the West to shape our entire culture.[28] Contrary to the prevailing idea that Turner's thesis helps to explain the development of American institutions, it is the current of myth and symbol already widely accepted by Americans that accounts for the wide acceptance of the thesis formulated by Turner. Thus Smith argues convincingly that Turner's thesis, instead of explaining the development of American institutions, is itself explained by the dominant image and myth of the American West. Indeed, the myth of the garden is the very animating source of Turner's thesis. "The idea of nature suggested to Turner a poetic account of the influence of free land as a rebirth, a regeneration, a rejuvenation of man and society constantly recurring where civilization came into contact with the wilderness along the frontier."[29]

Smith is attempting a totally new kind of historical approach in *Virgin Land*, treating written history itself on the same methodological level as literature, that is, as an act of the imagination. The dynamic synthesis of imagination and theory made by Turner is, moreover, not restricted to history alone. In *Virgin Land* Smith repeatedly documents his contention that myth also infuses social, political, and economic theory as a structural principle.

This idea is one that Smith shares with Northrop Frye, who was struck by a similar insight with regard to Freud's Oedipal theory. Frye goes a step further than Smith and draws an analogy between myth and mathematics. Mathematics appears to be a kind of informing or structural principle in the natural sciences. It continually gives shape and coherence to them without being itself involved in any kind of external proof or evidence. Is it not possible, Frye goes on, that myth is similarly a structural principle in the social or qualitative sciences, giving shape and coherence to psychology, anthropology, theology, history, and political theory?[30] For example, Freud's hypothesis of an Oedipus complex has been taken as an explanation for the dramatic effectiveness of a conflict theme in literature, as in a like manner Turner's thesis was taken as an explanation for the growth of American democracy. Is it not possible, then, that it is the myth that explains the power of these hypotheses over men's minds? This is one meaning that seems to come out of Smith's discussion. And it suggests that some of the deeply rooted theoretical assumptions of the social sciences can be approached from an entirely new perspective. Since they themselves may be animated by cultural myths, explanatory hypotheses of the social sciences may give information about a culture entirely apart from their ability to explain specific classes of cultural phenomena. The "basic" styles of the social sciences (in Pearce's language) demand investigation from American Studies.

In spite of the achievements of Smith's work, several problems, which grow out of his discussion, need to be considered. Certainly Smith has fulfilled his own request for a method that can cope with a broad range of cultural phenomena. But he does not, I believe, meet his equally important demand for a comprehensive method that will deal adequately with the most important writers of a culture.

Attacking the methods of the quantitative approach to culture, Smith points out the "relative homogeneity of popular art" that "lends itself to the quantitative methods of content analysis." But, he asks, "is nothing of consequence about a culture to be learned from its serious art? I suppose that when we speak of a serious novel, for example, we have in mind a work whose meaning is not exhausted by the identification of stereotyped ideas and attitudes in it."[31] The knowledge we have of a culture would be incomplete, indeed it would be radically false, Smith implies, if the serious work of a period is not taken into account. "Subtract the work of a few dramatists from what we know of Periclean Athens, or of Elizabethan England, and our image of the culture undergoes a drastic change, quite apart from merely aesthetic considerations."[32] But Smith's recognition of the definitive role of the best artistic productions in characterizing a period, such as the Elizabethan Age, is not carried through. A historian of American culture from a vantage point of four centuries in the future would surely give a different reading of the dominant myth of nineteenth-century America if he based his interpretation on the most serious writers of that century: Walt Whitman, James Fenimore Cooper, Henry David Thoreau, Mark Twain, and Herman Melville to recall only a few. Of these five men Smith discusses only Whitman and Cooper in detail. Are we to assume then that they are more "significant" than Thoreau and Melville? Even if this were granted, neither of these artists is a supporter of the myth of the garden. Walt Whitman is interpreted by Smith as exemplifying the myth of the passage to India; the central figure in Cooper's work is Leatherstocking, the model of the frontiers-man symbol. Neither Whitman's myth nor Cooper's symbol, on the basis of Smith's reading of the evidence, was the dominant or characteristic myth of the nineteenth century.

What of the other three men? How significant does Smith consider Thoreau, Twain, and Melville? The index of *Virgin Land* contains two references to Thoreau (only one of which carries over to a second page) and two references to Melville — one of them five pages long, the other only two pages long. Twain, who has been singled out by Smith as a special interest, receives only four references — only one of which is more than a one- or two-line citation. Other equally serious nineteenth-century American writers receive no greater attention from Smith. Hawthorne is not mentioned at all. The reader is led to suspect that the "significance" of a writer in *Virgin Land* may depend upon the ability of the author to extrapolate the kind of reading that will support his thesis.

To make the significance of literature contingent upon a criterion which is nonaesthetic raises the same paradox that we saw in *The Continuity of American Poetry*. Some great literature becomes insignificant in terms of the nonaesthetic criterion, and some mediocre, or at most good, literature becomes highly significant. There is nothing intrinsically misleading about a nonaesthetic criterion if it is used for nonaesthetic purposes. But when a nonaesthetic criterion is substituted for an aesthetic one and the significance of literature is judged in terms of it alone, systematic distortion of judgment takes place. Smith has a healthy aversion to this type of distortion, but the danger nevertheless lingers.

The second large issue suggested by *Virgin Land* was also raised by *The Continuity of American Poetry*: cultural isolationism. Since this seems to be a problem intrinsic to holism itself, the discussion of it in chapter I applies *mutatis mutandis* to Smith's holistic assumptions. Smith, like Pearce, unhesitatingly uses themes and motifs which connect the myths and symbols of his discussion to the larger scene of world myth and legend: the hero, the quest, and the millennium in which Time has ceased its flow. The idea of a continental empire as a passage to India was part of an older legendary belief in an inevitable succession of empires which rise and fall, always moving west. This tradition was expressed in Bishop Berkeley's melancholy utterance: "Westward the course of empire takes its way."[33] Similarly, it is not just the name "the myth of the garden" which relates the myth of an agrarian utopia to the millennial quests for a promised land in all ages. The quest for a new Eden is explicit in the writings of many men quoted by Smith.[34] As Smith, Pearce, and Lewis each point out, terms like *Adamic, garden, paradise,* and *passage to India* were not used arbitrarily by themselves, but were used, quite self-consciously, in many places by the authors of the nineteenth century.

But like Pearce, Smith avoids discussing the cross-cultural aspects of myth. The restrictions imposed by the area of research only partially explain this aversion. It may, in fact, be dictated by the author's holistic commitment, which insists upon the insularity and uniqueness of culture and its phenomena.

IV

The Warrior -Politician as Cultural Hero: Ward's *Andrew Jackson, Symbol for an Age*

The Conceptual Framework:
Cultural Ideology and the Unity of Nature,
Providence, and Will

Unlike the other subjects of this book, John Ward is a historian rather than a literary critic. However, his book *Andrew Jackson, Symbol for an Age* (1955) is of special interest to literary critics as well as cultural historians for two reasons: Ward is concerned with the cultural dynamics of mythopoesis (or cultural symbol creation) and *Andrew Jackson* contains an implicit holistic theory of the genesis of myth; and the materials which form the basic data of his research and evidence lie on the periphery of products of the literary imagination: political speeches, eulogies, anecdotes, popular songs and poems, cartoons, satire, and popular folk legends.

In his preface Ward speaks of Henry Nash Smith's "pervasive" influence on his work.[1] Begun as a doctoral dissertation under Smith's supervision, Ward's book stands as a complement to *Virgin Land*. For us the important thing about *Andrew Jackson* is not simply that Ward's method derives from Smith's, but that it refines and extends the theory of mythopoesis that is assumed in *Virgin Land*. In spite of Ward's debt to Smith, his own work reflects sufficient methodological independence (indeed there are a number of important methodological differences) to warrant separate treatment of its own accomplishments.

The premise of Ward's book is that Andrew Jackson became the hero of his age in a much larger sense than has generally been recognized by students of American culture.[2] Jackson became, in fact, a symbol for an entire age — the age generally defined as the greater part of the first half of the nineteenth century. The question he proposes to answer is how and why people came to think of Jackson in the way they did — as a figure of heroic proportions. In answering this question, Ward devotes a surprisingly small portion of his book to Jackson the man. This fact is a clue to the central purpose of the author. It was not what Jackson was or did that made him into a symbol, for "the obvious fact [is] that historical actuality imposed little restriction on the symbolic role the people demanded Andrew Jackson to play."[3] Consequently Ward is primarily concerned with what contemporaries of Jackson thought Old Hickory was and did. And what they thought they saw in Jackson was actually a direct reflection of themselves. The task, therefore, that Ward sets for himself is to analyze those aspects of the American character, mind, and imagination which came together in a dynamic unified symbol in Jackson. It was a symbol with dramatic and psychological power, a symbol through which "were projected the age's leading ideas . . . nature, providence, and will."[4]

For the present, we can leave aside the dramatic unity of these central concepts and concentrate on the logical unity of Ward's analysis, which he identifies as cultural. By "logical coherence" he means that the "concepts, nature, providence, and will, are organically inter-related; they possess a . . . coherence which makes a whole and it is their total configuration that determines the symbol, Andrew Jackson."[5] Ward expresses the notions of coherence, wholeness, and the organic interrelation of ideas and symbol in still another way. The general concepts, nature, providence, and will, "are the structural underpinnings of the ideology of early nineteenth-century America, for which Andrew Jackson is *one* symbol."[6] These statements strongly suggest Ward's holistic orientation but some confusion arises from his failure to define the term *ideology,* which is, I believe, the key to his conceptual framework. In ordinary usage *ideology* is a vague term much like *myth*, but technically (especially since Karl Marx) it has had in the social sciences a specialized meaning which must be emphasized in order to appreciate the significance of Ward's concept of the cultural genesis of symbol and (in like manner) myth.

Leaving aside Marx's emphasis on class struggle and economic determinism, the general Marxian model of society may help shed some light on Ward's use of *ideology*. Marx argues that consciousness is existentially conditioned: "It is not the consciousness of men that determines their being, but, on the contrary, their social being that determines their consciousness."[7] Thought, then, and institutions are creations and reflections of an underlying material reality. Ideology, in relationship to the material processes which underlie it, is merely epiphenomenal. Nothing in the ideological superstructure can be understood independently of the material reality. The substructure of society produces a superstructure of institutions and beliefs that is a mirror image of its internal reality. The substructure determines the character of the conscious level of society including the character of intellectual life. Although academicians believe thought is primary, this is simply not so, according to Marx. There are two basic concepts related to Marx's theory of social structures that have pervaded contemporary social science and that throw light on Ward's *Andrew Jackson*: the relationship of cause and effect between the substructure and the superstructure and the mirroring of the substructure by the superstructure.*

The substructure determines in some absolute sense the ideological superstructure of society. This implies the organic unity of society and suggests that human action (and even thought) is extrapersonal and conditioned by the social reality out of which it grows. Change in the superstructure comes about only through a prior change in the substructure and reflects the substantive change. Modes of expression on the level of superstructure are organically related to one another functionally as they are related to the substructure functionally. Ward is not a Marxist; moreover, he is not an economic determinist and indeed exhibits relatively little interest in the causal forces that underlie

*These concepts have been perhaps more influential among European sociologists than among their American colleagues. I am thinking particularly of Karl Mannheim's *Ideology and Utopia* (New York, 1936) as well as the school of thought called the "sociology of knowledge."

the ideological modes of the Jacksonian period. But he has adopted a structural model for his discussion in *Andrew Jackson* that is similar to the Marxian model.

Ward is chiefly concerned, like Pearce and Smith, with the ideological commitments of culture, particularly its values, but also with the institutional embodiment of those values in their political forms. The three concepts around which the ideological commitments of early nineteenth-century America clustered were nature, providence, and will. Ward, as we have seen, calls these general concepts the "structural underpinnings" of the ideology of the society.[8] He means by this that specific and identifiable beliefs about nature, providence, and will formed the ideological content of the Jacksonian period and from these three concepts flowed the energy which gave the ideology its dynamic thrust and eventuated in the creation of Andrew Jackson — the symbol.

One of the most important things about these concepts is that they have a "dramatic unity; that is, all three achieve realization through one figure."[9] Ward's theory of cultural symbol making, i.e., the process through which this realization comes about, will be taken up in detail later. It is enough at present simply to repeat Ward's point: "The symbolic Andrew Jackson is the creation of his time. Through the age's leading figure were projected the age's leading ideas. Of Andrew Jackson the people made a mirror for themselves."[10]

Ward's Use of Myth: Image, Symbol, and the Popular Imagination

The mythic qualities of the symbolic Andrew Jackson are suggested again and again in Ward's treatment of Jackson as an epic-cultural hero. Yet inasmuch as Ward only once specifically uses the term *mythology* in his study, Henry Nash Smith's view of the relationship between myth and symbol bears recalling here. Smith, it will be remembered, uses the words *myth* and *symbol* to refer to the same kinds of things.[11] The distinction between myth and symbol lies in their comprehensiveness: a myth involves a cluster of symbols and contains a narrative content. Ward differs from Smith chiefly in not making such a distinction. This failure is not inappropriate, for Ward, unlike Smith, is dealing only indirectly with large culture-coordinating myths which exhibit continuity over long periods of time, e.g., the myth of the garden of the world. Accordingly, when Ward speaks of symbol, we should understand that he designates a representation or image with mythic qualities.

To Ward, a symbol is created by the society and is a creation of its time. What seems to happen is that the individual becomes acculturated by internalizing society's demands into his own consciousness. Through this process of acculturation, the society's dominant values are assimilated by the individual and somehow projected into a symbol. The general concepts of nature, providence, and will simply underlie a number of specific cultural values. "But abstractions are not generally effective instruments of persuasion. It is for this reason that society creates its symbols. Symbols make abstract ideals concrete. One of the functions of the popular image of Andrew Jackson was to give substance to [abstractions]."[12] A symbol objectifies beliefs that are already held by a society. Jackson became a symbol, then, because of certain existing, necessary, and sufficient conditions for his elevation to the status of a cultural hero of epic proportions.

Jackson's victory at the Battle of New Orleans transformed his name at once into a household word. Ward isolates the beliefs and conditions making the transformation possible from a speech by Representative George Troup of Georgia in praise of Jackson:

1. "The victory at New Orleans was a victory of the American farmer." A causative relation is implied "between the life of the farmer and the victory of the American husbandman over Europe's finest." The farmer draws his strength from his deep and continuous association with nature.

2. "God is on our side; not only the God of Battles but God and Nature . . . have shown their special concern for the United States by the bountiful means placed at America's disposal."

3. "Will, the process of self-determination, brought victory to our side. Despite the seeming odds, an exertion of the self conquered and did the impossible."[13]

These beliefs about nature, providence, and will formed the ideological conditions for the conversion of Jackson to a symbol.

Further, as Ward has stated, the Jackson symbol was so effective it organically related the three concepts into a dynamic unity. This transformation Ward analyzes in the context of popular and folk art. Popular art is produced specifically for mass consumption: popular songs, political cartoons, political humor, and speeches. Folk art is more or less spontaneous creativity which is not conscious of itself as creative or artistic: nicknames, many political slogans, folk songs, and many spontaneous metaphors. Both are of equal importance in Ward's study.

The immediate aftermath of New Orleans was a profound and spontaneous outpouring of praise for Jackson. The War of 1812 had been a dreary failure for the American people and this one victory, even though it came after the treaty with the British had already been signed, saved American pride from a disastrous collapse. It also propelled Jackson to the level of a national hero and in the minds of the people a hero he remained.

The place held by Jackson in the minds of the people is suggested by the song "The Hunters of Kentucky," introduced by Noah M. Ludlow in 1822:

> "But Jackson he was wide awake, and
>   wasn't scared with trifles,
> For well he knew what aim we take
>   with our Kentucky rifles;
> So we marched us down to 'Cyprus Swamp';
>   The ground was low and mucky;
> There stood 'John Bull,' in martial pomp,
>   *But here was Old Kentucky.*"[14]

The response to this popular song was so incredible one must conclude that something profoundly gripping and significant about the country was being expressed.[15] Through some cultural process, this song embodied the whole complex of ideas and beliefs of a vast number of the people.

We have already seen this process in the discussion of Pearce in chapter II. Language is the carrier and center of culture. The power of language lies in its ability to symbolize. As Leslie White says, "Articulate speech is the most important form of symbolic expression."[16] But clearly language is not the sole form of symbolic expression nor is it necessarily the most important for the mythic imagination. There is also art, and this includes popular art and folk art. We may take cartoons as a paradigm. The eminent art historian E. H. Gombrich, writing of "The Cartoonist's Armoury," points out that when we study cartoons we also study symbols in a "circumscribed context." Cartoonists present us with metaphors. "It is the strength . . . of the cartoonist that . . . he makes it easier for us to treat abstractions as if they were tangible realities. . . . One of the things the study of cartoons may reveal with greater clarity is the role and power of the mythological imagination in our political thought and decisions. Historically this is obvious. For the so-called personifications, which cartoonists can so rarely do without, are the direct descendants of the ancient Olympians."[17] The thrust of Gombrich's statement is that in cartoons we see the symbolical and mythological imagination at work, presenting us with metaphors and other images that somehow capsulate abstract ideas. The process by which this imagination works Gombrich calls "condensation," which is "the telescoping of a whole chain of ideas into one pregnant image."[18]

Ward analyzes two contemporary cartoons with Jackson as their subject to show how they presented the contrast between a dynamic republic nourished by nature and a corrupt monarchical government. One cartoon does this explicitly by attaching lines from Byron's *Childe Harold's Pilgrimage,* which praise America as undefiled nature and the champion of freedom. The second cartoon renders the contrast more implicitly, picturing Europe as a large masonry building and America as "a cornfield surrounded by a split rail fence." Both cartoons, according to Ward, implied that advanced civilization is decadent, that is, "material advancement is organically connected with political debility."[19] Throughout the entire period the British were called barbarians and vandals, and accused of "cruelty, lust and horrours unknown to civilized nations."[20] Americans, however, were "cultivated" by nature. Jackson was called a combination of both primitivism and civilization, symbolizing nature at its very best.[21] The savage primitivism of the forest was rejected on the one hand as the brutal civilization of Europe was rejected on the other. The Western pastoral is the setting for true civilization.

Ward's insight in *Andrew Jackson* subsumes Gombrich's suggestion and extends beyond cartoons to other forms of popular and folk art. In Ward's analysis, Jackson is the dominant image which "condenses" a lower cluster of images which in turn "telescope" a chain of concepts or ideas related to nature, providence, and will. We may conceive of this graphically as a pyramiding process with Jackson at the very top, personifying symbolically the major political and ideological concepts of the age.

Jackson, by linking the symbolic and mythical with the real, creates the fusion, the amalgam, that seems so powerful to the human imagination. The basic values of a culture are projected into its chosen hero who, then, by his dramatic personification of those values condenses them into an image of the entire culture which beholds him as its savior and a mirror image of itself.

It is this dramatic unity we must now examine in detail. As we have seen, "The Hunters of Kentucky" plumbed the deep well of an essential American experience. It also expressed the tacit premises of an American philosophy of nature. The song, in essence, suggested that Europe's finest soldiers, the same soldiers who had defeated Napoleon at Waterloo, were no match for the backwoods farmers who marched from their frontier homes to defend the city of New Orleans. The point Ward makes is that the song expressed symbolically a favorite American attitude toward nature as the cause of American superiority to Europe. No soldiers Europe could put in the field, it was believed, were the equals of the frontier farmer with his long musket. Ward presents overwhelming evidence to show the Americans had no such natural superiority at New Orleans. The mythologizing mind is, however, not constrained by facts. The myth operating here needs no further elaboration — it is the frontier pastoral myth of the garden discussed in the previous chapter. In the American mind, regardless of the historical order of facts, the frontiersman assured military victory at New Orleans because he lived as a natural man and thus had the power of nature behind him.[22] The victory was consequently a victory of Adamic man; it was the defeat of a corrupt civilization. The immensely successful "Hunters of Kentucky" functioned in the area of imaginative play as the cartoon does — it condensed a complex of ideas about nature and reflected the restored American pride in its natural superiority. Political speeches of the period expressed the same concept:

> The most obscure soldier in the American lines saw that the hour of peril was at hand, and instead of shrinking from the horrors of the approaching tempest, seemed by the cheerfulness of his countenance and the alacrity with which he obeyed the orders of his officers, to wait its coming with the composure and firmness that belongs to cultivated minds. This is not to be wondered at; they were almost to a man freeholders, or the sons of freeholders; they were not taken from the streets of dissipated and corrupt cities, or enlisted into the army to prevent their becoming victims to the shivering pangs of want.[23]

Like "The Hunters of Kentucky," this excerpt from a speech by Nathaniel H. Claiborne stresses the yeoman origins of the American troops. In addition, it rejects civilization as embodied by the "dissipated and corrupt cities" of Europe.

Andrew Jackson's canonization seemed to grow naturally out of the events at New Orleans. First, he was the commander. Second, his frontier origins were perfect preparation for the role he was to play. Contemporary accounts referred to him as "one of nature's noblemen."[24] This term implied a dynamic relationship between nature and a nobility which could be conferred neither by heredity nor by kings. Ward suggests that the attitude implied by America's philosophy, symbolized by Jackson, is not simply a rejection of Europe but a belief that Europe is the complete antithesis of nature: it is "not-nature. It [Jackson as a symbol] also lends itself to a preference for the natural over the artificial, the intuitive over the logical. . . ."[25]

Jackson's victory helped make him a national hero. More importantly, it established him as a cultural hero at the symbolic level. One of the functions of the hero is to coordinate his culture, as Jackson did in resolving the conflict between corrupt hyper-civilization and the wild frontier. As Ward points out, in Jackson's America the natural hero was the farmer: "The plow was his symbol and his weapon, the farm his realm, and the property deed his title to legitimacy."[26] True cultivation, personified by the symbol, Jackson, was a blend of nature and civilization.

Two major supports of Jacksonianism, says Ward, were nature and intuition — the doctrine of the inner light. The organic connection between nature and intuition is patent: actually intuition is part of the philosophy of nature. Nature is the source of natural law and truth and therefore of natural wisdom. The logic of the professor and the schoolmaster is artificial. Summing up his most important chapter on the concept of nature, Ward states:

> Andrew Jackson captured the American imagination at the
> Battle of New Orleans, which rightfully stands for the point in
> history when America's consciousness turned westward, away
> from Europe toward the interior. Jackson not only symbolized
> the negative side of this phenomenon, the rejection of the old
> world, but also its positive side, the formation of a philosophy
> of nature (of which the new world had a virtual monopoly)
> with the further implication of the intuitive character of
> wisdom. Andrew Jackson embodied the latter two concepts
> for the contemporary imagination. He was presented as a
> child of the forest and the major incidents of his career were
> explained in terms of his untutored genius.[27]

Thus Jackson's symbolic function was to personify the major ideological assumptions of his age. From the perspective of the previous chapter, he might be thought of as the central symbol in the great culture-coordinating myth of the nineteenth century: the myth of the garden.

The second major ideological concept involved in the canonization of Jackson as a culture hero is providence. The assumption that underlies this concept is simply that God intervened on Jackson's behalf (at New Orleans and afterward) because God or providence is on America's side. In some speeches in the period immediately after the battle at New Orleans, Jackson was identified as God's chosen agent. He was also called "the instrument of Heaven's merciful designs," and "the man of his [God's] right hand."[28] Countrywide, editorial writers were prone to see the hand of God in the events of the battle and to characterize Jackson as the instrument and earthly representative of heaven.

Americans, says Ward, almost universally thought of God as their special possession and Jackson himself "was accustomed to refer to his role in the victory as that of 'the humble instrument of a superintending Providence.' " Ward argues that "the widely shared belief that the victory over the British at New Orleans was the result of the intervention of providence is not due simply to the piety of the American people in the early nineteenth century; it is part of the enormous egotism evidenced in Francis Hopkinson's use of the possessive pronoun in referring to God ['To bless oúr God ...']. In a period of intense nationalism, Americans saw themselves as a latter-day chosen race and quite comfortably referred to God as 'ours.' "[29] This kind of anthropocentrism is, perhaps, not as unusual as Ward appears to suggest; it seems to be found in almost all cultures. What is truly significant, however, is that America's anthropocentrism was so invariably and markedly expressed through the image of Andrew Jackson. Throughout Jackson's life there were suggestions that Jackson, "who represented the will of the people, also represented the will of God." When, in 1835, an attempt upon Jackson's life failed, an editorialist explained that "Providence has ever guarded the life of the man who has been destined to preserve and raise his country's glory and maintain the cause of the people."[30]

A whole complex of symbolic devices suggesting heaven's favor developed around Jackson in folk and popular art. Cartoonists used lightning in cartoons about Jackson to suggest Jackson's close relationship with the forces of heaven. Symbols such as lightning, meteors, and whirlwinds confirmed Jackson's connection with both nature and providence and connected them dramatically to one another.

The notion of a culture hero favored by God who intervenes in his behalf is very common to myth. The hero is the savior of his culture; he brings order from chaos and with God's help he carries forth the mission of his society and helps to fulfill the destiny of his culture. Gregor Sebba, commenting upon the idea of mission, states: "If a nation feels its moral foundations or its independence threatened, if it is in search of a justification of its goals and policies, it may seek recourse in a myth ... [which] gives its endeavors moral sanction, or endows it with a superior 'mission.' ... [T]he myth of the historical mission may be quite strong when linked with ... good engaged in a ... struggle against the evil."[31]

The "destiny" of the United States in the nineteenth century in the popular and political minds of America was to regenerate and restore to man his lost rights. This destiny seemed manifest and the conjunction of those two words *manifest destiny* justified a century-long expansionist movement. Ward paraphrases one editorial writer who pointed out that "because providence had assigned the cause of freedom to the American people, legal decisions, precedents of international law, and merely logical objections to the expansion of the United States were . . . quite beside the point."[32]

Jackson's role in the expansionist movement was twofold. He was involved as an actor, and he symbolized "the underlying assumption which made expansion seem necessary and right."[33] In a speech in 1843 Jackson described expansion as "extending the area of freedom." This provided a handy rationalization for the expansionist movement. The belief that America should serve as an example to the rest of the world underlay the rising nationalism in two ways: "It made American isolation morally acceptable" and "It supported nearly any self-seeking national program by phrasing it in terms of the highest international altruism."[34] Andrew Jackson personally embodied both these aspects. It is worth quoting Ward at some length on Jackson's symbolization of these beliefs about providence, nature, and manifest destiny:

> He symbolized the special concern of providence for America which is the basic assumption of the various ideas grouped under the term, manifest destiny. Also, as we have seen, the presentation of Jackson as a child of nature embodied the concept which made it seem feasible and even necessary that America cut itself off from Europe. Lastly, it was Jackson himself who pointed out to his contemporaries how they could justify their acquisitiveness by subsuming it under the divine plan of providence manifestly indicated for all to see in the configurations of new world geography, so that nature and providence were intertwined at every turn. God was . . . "the God of nature and of nations."[35]

Clearly Andrew Jackson provides a connection between the concepts of nature and providence. "God and nature watched over the unique course of America's destiny; both were symbolized in the figure of Andrew Jackson."[36] This conjunction is what Gombrich has called the process of condensation in which two or more abstract concepts are telescoped into one symbol. If Jackson symbolized the philosophy of nature which underlay the American rejection of Europe, he also symbolized "the special favor of God which consecrated American expansion."[37]

The roots of the American ideology of individualism, according to Ward, may be found in the third idea embodied by Jackson: the concept of will. "The same pattern which one discovers in examining the concepts of nature and providence emerges when one scrutinizes Jackson's relation to the idea of the self-made man."[38] The idea of man as the author of his own fate was a traditional figure in American society. Jackson gave added support to an already established belief in America. Will, as it was embodied symbolically by Andrew Jackson, is suggested in the idea that although God was on Old Hickory's side, he actually had no need of God. "From the day of the Battle of New Orleans," says Ward, "the idea that the victory was due to Jackson alone was widely entertained."[39]

Ward has analyzed those aspects of the American character, mind, and imagination which brought together the concepts nature, providence, and will embodied in the image of Jackson in a dynamic twofold unity, a dramatic unity and an organic unity. The discussion of dramatic unity is one of his most important contributions since dramatic unity in an image is similar to what some writers have called a cultural image with a "strain toward the aesthetic." By aesthetic strain is meant "that there is a tendency for the vehicles of symbolic meaning, the true artifacts of culture, to take on aesthetic forms."[40] This aesthetic form is the quality that raises the symbol above chronological history, gives it its narrative and emotional richness, and thereby connects it to all myth.

Holism and Symbol in Andrew Jackson, Symbol for an Age

Several questions must now be raised. What is the relationship between culture, ideology, symbol, and value? What are the cultural forces which produce a symbol as powerful as Old Hickory? What is the relation of cultural symbols in general and the symbol Andrew Jackson in particular to the culture in which they are found?

Implicit in *Andrew Jackson* is an unspoken theory of cultural symbolization similar to that of Smith in *Virgin Land*: a theory of need. Why was the particular symbol Andrew Jackson produced at that particular moment in history? The immediate cause during the War of 1812, according to Ward, was that Jackson at New Orleans satisfied the desire of the American people to be purged of the shame and frustration of defeat. This single event, though important in the early stages of Jackson's canonization, was not the long-range cause, however. Need, not logic, determines belief, including the larger complexes of belief such as nature, providence, and will. For example, there is no logic in the American belief that God is on America's side and ensures her success. This belief, according to Ward, was the consequence of the need of a violently expanding nation for self-justification. Belief, then, functions to uphold a nation's self-assurance about the rightfulness of its goals and its actions to attain its goals.

Ward extends this idea to the theory of symbol formation itself. A society must develop the kind of character that will assure social conformity and belief in its social direction. In his discussion of Andrew Jackson and the concept of will, Ward turns to the social sciences for his point. The United States, he argues, solved "the problem of social direction by the development of a new character type. . . . [A]n expanding society internalizes its goals within each of its members, creating what the sociologist, David Riesman, calls the 'inner-directed' character."[41] What happens, according to Ward, is that society's demands are internalized by individuals in the society. Individuals then strive for society's goals which now seem to be their own personal goals. These goals are defined as values, such as "Work is good"; "Self-reliance is good"; "Europe is decadent." These and many other similar values constitute the three main ideological constructs of the mid-nineteenth century. Society, then, creates the ideological requirements which the individual internalizes as commitments and beliefs about reality (what MacIver calls dominant thought forms). These internalized commitments become goals for the individual.

This process is carried one step further. Since abstractions are not generally persuasive, "society creates" symbols, which give the abstract ideals a concreteness they could never otherwise attain. "One of the functions of the popular image of Andrew Jackson was to give substance to the abstraction, will."[42] Similarly one of the functions of the symbol Jackson was "to give substance" as well to the abstractions, or thought forms, nature and providence.

Now clearly Jackson as a cultural symbol not only functions to condense the abstract ideological commitments of the culture but is functionally reflexive in that it relates back to the culture in some specific way. Terms like *society creates* and *society produces an internalization of goals* imply that society in some way stands in a cause-effect relationship between its needs and the fulfillment of them. Need produces the symbol as well as the abstract ideological concepts. Like an organism, a society adjusts to its needs. One of the instruments of adjustment is the cultural symbol. Speaking of the role of the cultural hero, Ward comments, "For a society facing . . . [problems], the Hero is the one who brings order out of chaos by conquering nature; he is the boon-giver of civilization who ventures forth to bring back the power that reinvigorates the world."[43] Problems appear in the form of disorder, tensions, and ambivalences which destroy the balance of the social organism. In a holistic culture any imbalance or destruction of the social equilibrium registers throughout the whole system which then attempts to adjust. It is the society that produces its own resolution in the form of a symbol. The symbol is an imperative to action which resolves tension and restores the homeostatic balance of the whole.

The dynamic restorative power of the symbol is the result of two features: its ability to mirror the society and its rich dramatic content. Of Andrew Jackson, says Ward, "the people made a mirror for themselves."[44] This mirror analogy is common in the social sciences. Many anthropologists take for granted that the beliefs, the myths, and, in general, the ideas of primitive peoples are a reflection of their social structures.[45] Jackson is a "mirror" for the society since he embodies the beliefs and goals which are first internalized by the people and then projected out again into a symbolic form. The form and content of the symbol may or may not conform to historical reality. But the question of whether it does or not is irrelevant as Ward so often reminds us.

We are dealing with an imaginative emotional construction in which belief has been transformed into an image of great dramatic power. This emotional content is particularly important, for it is the source of the power to reinforce social and cultural goals and values. Since abstractions have no such efficacy in supporting cultural values and action, it is the myths and symbols of a culture that are the true source of cultural continuity. The symbol emotionally engages the internalized values of the culture, informing and confirming belief.

The entire system of relations is a functioning whole. Social needs are expressed in abstract ideological commitments internalized by individual members of the society. The commitments are projected in a symbol which condenses the abstract ideas and reflexively confirms the truth of cultural beliefs, engages the emotions of individuals, and promotes action to fulfill social need. MacIver's words bear repeating here with a simple substitution of *symbol* for his term *myth.* "We have pointed out that all social relations — the very texture and the very being of society — are [symbol] sustained, and that all changes of the social structure are mothered and nurtured by appropriate new [symbols]."[46] From the shelter of symbol man perceives and experiences the world.

Ward's theoretical assumptions are unsurprisingly similar to those of Henry Nash Smith. It is accordingly no surprise that at many points their works are closely parallel. The vision of culture presented by both writers is that of a functionally integrated whole in which value, belief, myths, symbols, and rites, however extraordinary, fulfill cultural needs just as, for example, hunger fulfills a need for the biological organism. Like Smith, Ward is more deeply interested in what people *thought* their history was than what the chronology of empirical facts actually was. People view the world and themselves from the shelter of ideology through the lens of myth. These assumptions place Ward fully within the framework of holism.

Accomplishments and Problems

Ward has added significantly to our understanding of the remarkable period of American history we have traditionally called the age of Jackson. As Ward so accurately points out, "To describe the early nineteenth century as the age of Jackson misstates the matter. The age was not his. He was the age's."[47] Ward has shown us the process through which Jackson became the symbol of the age. Equally important, however, Ward has refined and added to the developing American Studies methodology.

In many ways, as we have seen, *Andrew Jackson* follows the methods explored by Henry Nash Smith in *Virgin Land.* Ward's unique contribution is his applied elaboration of the connection between ideology and cultural symbolism or myth. The tendency of many writers is either to confuse ideology and myth with one another or to deny there is any connection at all.

The tendency to confuse ideology and myth seems to have its roots in the fact that both terms signify to many a common set of characteristics which have negative connotations — connotations approximating deceit or self-deceit, or at any rate, signifying an interested or subjective approach to reality, an attitude going off on a tangent to truth. In contrast, then, a word like *science* usually implies an objective, disinterested approach to reality, entirely harmonious with truth. When myth and ideology are confused, the result is the kind of identification made by Leslie White between the cultural hero and the ideology of the culture. (See chapter I.)

Few writers have attempted to explore the possible connections between ideology and myth. Karl Marx is silent on the entire subject of myth. Ben Halpern remarks on the extraordinary insularity of the major writers who comment on the two concepts. Mannheim does not once refer to Ernst Cassirer, Sir James Frazer, Bronislaw Malinowski, Max Mueller, or Gilbert Murray. Cassirer's *Essay on Man* makes no mention of Mannheim, Georg Lukacs, Ernst Troeltsch, or Max Weber. Susanne Langer has no references to Friedrich Engels, Georg Lukacs, Karl Mannheim, Karl Marx, Thorstein Veblen, or Max Weber.[48] It would be absurd to conclude that the great writers on myth like Cassirer and Langer were not familiar with their counterparts and that Mannheim did not know well the work of the great scholars on myth. It may be that each group felt the writings of the other to be irrelevant to its own concerns. Only recently have social psychologists and others begun to insist on the close connection of ideology and myth, and controversy still boils around the subject. Ward may well be the first writer to attempt to bring the combined concepts to bear on a historical problem.

Although Ward's contributions to American Studies methodology are significant, his work raises both practical and theoretical problems. In emphasizing Jackson's symbolic importance for an entire age, Ward naturally stresses the harmonious factors contributing to the creation of the symbol and, as a result, minimizes the importance of conflict and discrepancy. Nowhere does he indicate the size of the majorities which Jackson achieved at the polls; yet this would seem to be of some significance in establishing Jackson's relationship to his age. Actually, Jackson failed to receive a majority vote in 1824 (there are reliable statistics on the popular vote for this election). In his successful campaigns of 1828 and 1832 approximately 56 percent of the electorate voted for him, [49] hardly the landslide we would expect for a man having such a powerful symbolic impact. It is tempting to envision Jackson as a cultural symbol because he seemed to be the innovator of a new era. Yet one problem cannot be avoided: why did very sizable numbers reject Jackson at the polls? Why did so many Americans not respond to the symbol? Did they not share in the values and attitudes discussed by Ward?

Ward makes only three brief references to the attacks made on Jackson by his opponents. The Whigs referred to their antagonist as a barbarian, the product of unbridled nature;[50] they charged that he was dominated by the men around him, that he was *not* a man of strong will;[51] and they argued that Jackson was a military chieftain who placed himself beyond the law as a threat to a free society.[52] Obviously, these references support Ward's claim that Jackson's opponents shared the same attitudes as his friends, although they interpreted Jackson differently. But such charges are not the only ones made against Jackson; they are simply the only ones which conform to Ward's schematization. Jackson was also attacked as immoral for living in adultery and frequently derided as a manipulator of the people, a man interested only in satisfying his personal ambitions, an unprincipled seeker of wealth. It is Jackson and his followers to whom one contemporary critic referred when he wrote of the parties then in vogue which, instead of serving the people, ministered to the "avarice, ambition, or pride of some temporary idol, who is worshipped one day and immolated on the next."[53] Surely Ward could have found much more evidence of diversity had he so desired. But such evidence may have confuted much of his argument. Jackson as a symbol is perhaps not as clearly defined as Ward's evidence would lead us to believe.

Another problem in establishing Jackson's status as a cultural symbol is rooted in the difficulty of determining precisely what Jackson represented to the people. Jackson's career reveals a number of inconsistencies. Except for the bank problem he seems to have had few strong feelings about the political issues of his day. It is not possible to assign Jackson the role of defending traditional pastoral values without serious reservations. In their best political rhetoric, Democrats claimed to be preserving the self-reliance of the yeoman and the right to equal opportunity. But a flavor of individualism somewhat different from their yeoman predecessors persists among the Jacksonians. They do not seem concerned about the right to own land, to be independent of their neighbors, to keep their families close to the soil. Theirs is the individualism of the land speculator, the small proprietor, the energetic young lawyer. Nowhere is this spirit more evident than in the attack on the Second National Bank. The bank was charged with favoritism toward the few, with granting special privileges which allowed some people to begin the race for success and riches with a head start. The Jacksonian individualist is imbued with an air of confidence that he can prevail over his competitor in a fair fight. Even though Democrats talked of self-reliance in a typically Jeffersonian way, they emphasized different aims. They wanted business to be completely divorced from government; they wanted to be free to pursue their own economic interests.[54]

The bank issue also brought to Jackson's support a variety of men prominent in state banks who envied the control exercised by the National Bank. Most Democrats would have vehemently denied that the controversy involved a contrast between the "outs" and the "ins." But this factor was surely present.[55] In vetoing the bill to recharter the hated Bank, Jackson himself condemned the use of government power to reward favored people.[56] Yet he owed much of his success as a political leader to the development of a highly disciplined faction which rewarded friends and punished enemies. In spite of the democratic rhetoric, Jacksonians were adept at developing and using political techniques designed to support their best interests in an expanding economy. If they did not boast of progress and science and industry as optimistically as the Whigs, they were nonetheless quicker than their opponents at capitalizing on the new uses of power.

The validity of Jackson as a cultural symbol is further clouded by the way his personal life could be seen by Americans as an example of either of the two conflicting value systems of the day. It is not likely that many Americans belonged wholeheartedly to either the traditionalist or the acquisitive faction. Most simply felt pulls toward both. No matter which pole exerted the greatest force, the individual could find elements in Jackson's life which accorded with either image. His military career could be interpreted as a badge of honor and devotion to country comparable to Washington's or it could be seen as an inordinate attempt to seize great personal power. His attack on the Bank could be interpreted as an effort to restore agrarian self-reliance or it could be understood as a move to break the bonds of privilege which restrained the people in their pursuit of material wealth. As a planter and large landholder, he might be considered something of an aristocrat who enjoyed life without striving for money or prestige; or this same piece of historical evidence might suggest that he was a land speculator and business adventurer who was caught up in the competitive struggle. Americans deeply committed to either value system might see Jackson as a man like themselves. The majority of Americans were probably gratified to see in Jackson a man who shared their personal ambitions yet were also anxious to find in him the virtues which they felt slipping from their grasp. Jackson's appeal to the imagination of his contemporaries may well have depended upon the flexibility which his life permitted each individual in coming to grips with the anxieties created by America's increasing materialism.

This discussion about Jackson's power over the popular mind is purely speculative, but it suggests the kinds of questions which should have been explored by Ward. The analysis of the value conflict in Jacksonian America is precisely the point to which Marvin Meyers addressed himself in *The Jacksonian Persuasion.*[57] Meyers sifted through his source material, found an overriding concern dominating the period, and structured his image of the era in terms of a struggle between two opposite forces. Ward approached the period through the single symbol: Andrew Jackson. His thesis, like that of Pearce and Smith, is, to a large extent, self-justifying and dictates the evidence to be presented. All historical scholarship, of course, is selective, but this prima facie truth should not be taken to mean that contrary evidence should not be explored.

By now the second problem — cultural isolationism — is too familiar to need further elaboration here. Ward's concept of the ideological determination of symbol implies a cultural insularity just as strong as that of Smith. Yet Ward, like Smith and Pearce, freely uses traditional mythical language in describing his material: the hero and the monster (in this instance the Bank), the traditional role of the hero, the association of the hero with the favor of the gods (providence). No theory of cultural determinism will fully explain these repetitive themes and motifs in culture after culture throughout history.

V

Culture and the Dramatic Dialogue: Lewis's *The American Adam*

The Conceptual Framework: Dialogue, Dialectic, and Holism

In *The American Adam* (1955) R. W. B. Lewis is concerned, like Pearce, with the Adamic myth. He hopes to identify "the beginnings and the first tentative outlines of a native American mythology."[1] The period covered by Lewis is primarily 1820-1860, although some of the most important works he discusses were finished long after 1860: *Billy Budd* (completed by Melville in 1891) and several novels by Henry James which furnish Lewis with a long list of evidence.

The native American mythology which Lewis identifies revolves around the figure of an American Adam. He suggests that the myth has three major characteristics: (1) The world in the mythic vision was just starting up again after having fumbled its first chance in the Old World. It "saw life and history as just beginning." (2) A new hero, in fact "a new kind of hero," came into being for the American myth. (3) The myth insisted that the New World itself was entirely new and had no connection with Europe's history or habits.[2] New human ideals and new human habits were to be engendered in the New World. A totally new personality embodied in a totally new image was envisaged. This was the new hero poised on the edge of the greatest human adventure. His characteristics paralleled those of the myth. The new hero was (1) "emancipated from history," (2) "happily bereft of ancestry," (3) "untouched and undefiled by the usual inheritances of family and race," (4) "an individual standing alone, self-reliant," (5) "ready to confront whatever awaited him," (6) "prior to experience," (7) "in his very newness . . . fundamentally innocent."[3]

Lewis sets out to examine the image and the myth. What were the impulses which begot the myth? What shape did the myth take in its cultural manifestations? What was its meaning for the new American nation?

Somewhat submerged at first, says Lewis, the myth became more and more explicit: in the beginning it was "the concealed cause of an ethical polemic, and it lurked behind the formal structure of works of fiction."[4] Lewis points out that not everyone counted as an unmixed blessing the newborn innocence in the American character and the American ideal which the image reflected. Indeed the reactions to the ideal are what set off a cultural debate which lasted to the end of the century and beyond. The voices in this debate are designated by Lewis as three: "the party of Hope" — those in full accord with the Adamic image; "the party of Memory" — those totally opposed to the image; and "the party of Irony" — those who were "skeptically sympathetic toward both parties and managed to be confined by neither."[5] These parties differed in their vision of man. The vision of each may be summarized in one word — Hope: innocence; Memory: sinfulness; Irony: tragedy.

One of the central themes in *The American Adam* is that the deep belief in the fundamental innocence of man in the "New World" of the American continent was the imaginative nourishment that produced the luxuriant growth in American letters. The literary flowering continued over the forty or so years before the fratricidal strife of the Civil War began to put an end to the belief. At this time the millennial vision of perfected man in a new Eden, a fundamental part of the belief in American innocence, also began to fade. The exhaustion of the vision of a new Adam — an American Adam — meant loss of a vital source of creativity. The disturbing part of this for Lewis is that no source of creativity of equal vitality has replaced the belief in innocence. He often suggests that the real importance of his work is that it charts the future as well as sounds the past. "Recent literature has applauded itself for passing beyond the childlike cheerfulness of Emerson and Whitman," but it has also lost the tragic understanding of Hawthorne or Melville.[6] "A century ago, the challenge . . . was an expressed belief in achieved human perfection, a return to the primal perfection. Today the challenge comes rather from the expressed belief in achieved hopelessness."[7] The contemporary situation is not as hopeless as we might suppose, however, for Lewis still sees the chance for new and "stirring impulsions." Nevertheless, the present cultural situation is a result of the exhaustion of an older impulsion.

This idea of a pattern, a rhythm, in the movement of culture is explicit in much, and implicit in all, of Lewis's discussion of the development of an American mythology. The idea of patterned cultural development — more particularly the notion of an impulse which dominates large groups of men or complexes of ideas or areas of creative development — is by now familiar as one of the characteristics exhibited by holism.

In his "Prologue," Lewis suggests that the history of a culture has its analogue in the "unfolding course of a dialogue." It is a dialogue that is "philosophic in nature," and it is carried on by several voices much as were Plato's dialogues. In American culture these are the voices of Hope, Memory, and Irony. As it develops, every culture seems to produce its own special and determining debate. The debate is conducted on the loftiest levels of the culture in its literature and thought, but is inseparable from the society's primary ideological concerns which preoccupy the culture at every level.

This debate, argues Lewis, is the highest level of culture because a culture actually achieves identity through the emergence of its particular dialogue. It is not the dominance of one set of ideas or convictions that distinguishes a culture, but the ideas which are held in tension through the dialogue. This is important methodologically because historians of ideas have too often, as Lewis sees, declared one or the other of the parties of Hope or Memory as the embodiment of the American character. They have usually completely neglected the party of Irony and hence have missed the interplay of ideas and the dramatic tension of the dialogue. Indeed, it is this dialogical tension, this opposition, this dialectic of ideas which tends to move the culture as it carries the debate forward. The historian should, therefore, approach the task of writing works in the history of ideas by looking "not only for the major terms of discourse, but also for major pairs of opposed terms which, by their very opposition, carry discourse forward. The historian looks, too, for the coloration or discoloration of ideas received from the sometimes bruising contact of opposites."[8]

According to Sidney Hook in *Reason, Social Myths, and Democracy,* one of the most important characteristics of dialectic is interrelatedness. Used in social inquiry, this is the method that has led, since the time of Hegel, to the perception that certain cultural patterns and ideals are so pervasive that a sharp separation of the fields of literature, religion, politics, and economics from each other makes unintelligible the structure, the problems, and to some extent the history of those fields.[9] As we have seen, holism similarly assumes that there can be no such separation. In both cases the reasons are the same. There are no "atomic facts" to be known, for every "fact" is related to another "fact" so that a branch of endeavor forms a whole. In a like manner, these wholes have an internal organic relation to one another. All wholes are related to each other in the same way as the parts of any whole are related to each other. If the configuration of these wholes is called "style," as it is in *The Continuity of American Poetry,* then the interrelated cultural wholes form the "life style" of the culture.

In *The American Adam* the interrelatedness of facts is a dialectical relation. The facts Lewis deals with are ideas, and they are connected by their reciprocal "opposition." A few of the most important pairs of opposed terms of the dialogue are innocence-experience, novelty-tradition, innocence-sin, good-evil, the present-the past.[10] It is the clash of these ideas in dramatic opposition that charts cultural change and growth.

The notion of process and growth is the second characteristic of dialectic that relates it to holism. One of the most common traditional conceptions of dialectic is that it is the pattern of existential change. This pattern is conceived not as a methodological construction but as a process which inheres objectively in both the natural and the social worlds. The dialectical process itself carries the culture forward in some determining pattern. Lewis suggests that the process is a growth "toward maturity" without ever defining precisely what "maturity" might include.[11] Two things about it should be singled out, however. The notion of growth toward maturity is another connection with holism, for it specifically designates the common analogy between culture and a living organism which was discussed in detail in chapter I. Second, the advance toward maturity is characterized by the emergence of a "native American mythology." Lewis does not tell his readers in his discussion of methodology what the source of the material of myth might be. He leaves this to be gleaned from the analytical development in the body of his work. But the very language in which he frames his discussion suggests the organic nature of culture. The fruit of the dialectical clash of ideas is a myth − a myth containing an image unique to American culture and consequently, in some sense, containing the distilled essence of American culture. Lewis is not interested in this myth on all levels of culture, only on the level of the imagination as the myth at that level has expressed itself in serious literature and thought. "My intention . . . is to disentangle from the writings and pronouncements of the day the emergent American myth and the dialogue in which it was formed. The American myth . . . [was] not fashioned . . . by a single man of genius. It was and it has remained a collective affair; it must be pieced together out of an assortment of essays, orations, poems, stories, histories, and sermons."[12]

At the early stages of cultural growth there is no question of the myth being in one piece. It is pieced together by Lewis himself. The center of consciousness is Lewis. Those early writers who fall under his eye are unaware of themselves as mythmakers. As the culture matures, however, the myth becomes more and more clearly articulated until in works like *The Marble Faun* and *The Golden Bowl* the myth becomes the actual model for narrative.[13] What this part of Lewis's argument clearly suggests, then, is that the myth at the "loftiest level" of culture reflects deeper levels of human existence in the world. The myth − the image of the American Adam in all its pristine purity − had, as the dialogue progressed, gained a hold on the consciousness and the imagination of American writers. Eventually cultural reality comes to be perceived under its form. This is particularly evident in works of the pure imagination, since "while the vision may be formulated in the orderly language of rational thought, it also finds its form in a recurring pattern of images — ways of seeing and sensing experience."[14] At this point, the myth itself has gained a power, an energy of its own. The imagery and the story "give direction and impetus to the intellectual debate itself; and they may sometimes be detected, hidden within the argument, charging the rational terms with unaccustomed energy."[15]

This energy is the galvanic source of the continuous development of the culture. Once the myth has reached its full stature and the most articulate members of the culture have become conscious of it as a model and as an issue for debate, the culture has reached its full maturity.

Lewis's Concept of Myth: The Authentic American as a New Adam

Lewis tells us that he is primarily concerned with the history of ideas, but he is especially interested, he adds, "in the representative imagery and anecdote that crystallized whole clusters of ideas."[16] The kind of image he is talking about is capable of embodying as a metaphorical vehicle the ideas that are distinctive about a culture. Lewis finds that "a century ago, the image contrived to embody the most fruitful contemporary ideas was that of the authentic American as a figure of heroic innocence and vast potentialities, poised at the start of a new history."[17] This is the image around which clustered those opposed sets of ideas of the cultural dialogue which gave American culture its identity.

Lewis explains the context in which he is using words like *myth* and *mythology* by suggesting a comparison with the Roman myth as it took shape ultimately in the *Aeneid* of Virgil. The *Aeneid* "was unmistakably a dramatization on a vast scale of the humanistic ideas set forth and debated in the philosophical dialogues of Cicero, two or three decades earlier." In his dialogues, Cicero brought together all the conflicting opinions of the contemporary Roman philosophical schools. Thus "Cicero discovered *the* dialogue of his generation."[18] Virgil ultimately created the myth which embodied the cultural dialogue.

What Virgil did was to impart to the Ciceronian view of things the energy it needed in order to form a vision of life for the Romans.

There seem to be two substantial differences between the Roman myth and the American myth: the number of people involved in the mythopoesis and the degrees of self-consciousness involved in the creations. Lewis insists that one man − Virgil − "consciously created" the Roman myth. However, the American myth was "emergent," it grew. It must be "disentangle[d] from the writings and pronouncements of the day." It is not simply *there*, clearly stated by a "single man of genius."[19] It was a collective affair, and, as we have seen, has to be pieced together by the historian.

Lewis's view of the myth raises a question: how does it emerge? Does Lewis mean simply that if we examine the evidence carefully as he has done, we will be able to help the myth take shape and emerge from the dialogue? Or does he not mean that somehow from the very intellectual and social soil in which the writers lived and worked there grew the myth? If Lewis means the former, then is the historian not in Virgil's position as the true center of conscious myth-creation? In that case, Lewis's analogy between the Roman and American myths means no more than that Roman culture: Cicero: Virgil is analogous to American culture: x collection of writers: R. W. B. Lewis as historian. But surely he means something quite different. The historian only discovers the myth; he does not create it.

The central image of the myth, we should recall, is a full embodiment of the authentic American, the American Adam. But every American is potentially the authentic American, for this is the very meaning of the myth; he is the new man unhampered by any bonds, self-reliant, independent, untouched and undefiled, and fundamentally innocent. The entire cultural potential is actualized in reality in every American just as it is actualized ideally in the image. Every living American is the heroic center of the nineteenth-century Adamic myth. This places the emergence of the myth in a much wider context than that of the lofty dialogue alone; it is placed in the context of the widest possible preoccupation of American culture, of all its activities and of its most fundamental ideological conflicts. An example is American fiction itself, which, Lewis points out, "has regularly registered through its own peculiar symbols the changing contours of the continent and its history."[20] Myth grows out of the total cultural situation and not simply from a piecemeal accumulation of dialectical themes heaped up by the historian.

Holism and Myth in Lewis's Theoretical Framework

We should, by now, be able to reach some conclusions about the connection between myth and the total culture in Lewis's theoretical framework. The myth of a culture is the symbolic self-interpretation of the human beings who have created the culture – in this case, it is the symbolic image of a totally innocent, new man. The myth or system of symbolization has a pattern of growth and decline that can be traced by the historian. In *The American Adam* Lewis's intention is to illustrate the pattern of cultural growth in America "at least on its loftiest levels." Man responds, first of all, to his environment. However, man's sense of his environment in the New World was contingent on his sense of the Old World and of the past. If this had not been so, then his sense of being unique and living in a unique situation would not have existed. From the very beginning, then, to say that Americans had a sense of being unique is to say paradoxically that they had a sense of history. Only as history has been fully alive to Americans have Americans been fully alive to the unique choices which faced them in a wilderness continent.

This sense of uniqueness is projected in the central symbol of the myth: the American Adam. Man's response to the land is emphasized not only by Lewis's remark that fiction registers the contours and history of the continent but also in his discussion of Faulkner's *The Bear* in a 1951 article from the *Kenyon Review*. This article foreshadows *The American Adam*, for it contains all the central ideas in a highly developed form. Discussing the meaning of the hero's initiation experience in the Mississippi wilderness of the 1880s, Lewis comments: ". . . no doubt it is time now to remember the national and provincial boundaries within which Ike's [Isaac McCaslin's] initiation is undertaken. For like *Moby Dick, The Bear* is most in tune with primary and perennial rhythms of experience when it is most explicitly American."[2][1] Explaining what he means by "Americanness" a few lines later, he adds: "The frontier, as Turner and Constance Rourke were the first to make clear, was the major physical source of this uniquely American idea: the idea, I mean, of a new, unspoiled area in which a genuine and radical moral freedom could once again be exercised — as once, long ago, it had been, in the garden of Eden. . . ."[2][2]

Taken together, these two comments emphasize two theoretically crucial points: that the idea of uniqueness and innocence, and consequently the dialogue about the idea and the image that crystallized the idea, had a *physical source* and that the deeper a work of the imagination thrusts down into the culture where it was conceived, the closer it is related to the "primary," the "perennial," the universal that crosses all cultural boundaries. Yet only in a cultural setting does man have moral choices, and only in American culture did man's moral choices seem to regain universal meaning just as the frontier seemed so much a symbol of man's beginnings. In *The Bear,* the "central poetic insight" is an insight into something much larger; "it is an insight into the fertile and ambiguous possibility of moral freedom in the new world. . . . Faulkner has projected another compelling image, so striking elsewhere in American fiction, of the ethically undefined."[2][3] Here Lewis, like Smith, Pearce, and Ward, connects myth with values.

Values, then, are both cultural and universal. Values grow out of a culture as man is faced with choices in his own world. But man as a value-creating organism has faced similar problems in every culture in every age throughout history. Man's cultural environment simply gives new shape to the age-old problems of man in the world. The shapes given to the ancient themes by the New World are the main topic of discussion in *The American Adam.* The most important point that emerges from the discussion so far is Lewis's emphasis on both the cultural and cross-cultural aspects of the myth of the American Adam. But there are several conclusions to be drawn from Lewis's discussion about the pattern or shape the cultural myth takes.

First, there appears to be an early period of gestation in which an insight begins to take on a particular form of symbolic self-interpretation. An embryonic image begins to develop. This phase, after the War of 1812, corresponds on the loftiest level to those early stages during which, Lewis says, the Adamic image though "invoked often" still "remained somewhat submerged, making itself felt as an atmospheric presence, a motivating idea."[24] From the documents of the time, Lewis illustrates that writers and thinkers were building a case against the past. In Thoreau and Hawthorne this was expressed ritually as a purification rite. As the past was rejected, as the party of Memory began to lose its supremacy, a new image of the American character began to emerge. Whitman's visionary song in *Leaves of Grass* exemplifies the inception and emergence of the symbol of the American Adam. It "brought to its climax the many-sided discussion by which — over a generation — innocence replaced sinfulness as the first attribute of the American character."[25] It was during these years that the party of Hope became the dominant voice in the dialogue.

Below the loftiest level, at the level of human action, in a word, the level of the "physical source," the rejection of the past and the emergence of a new vision of innocence in nature correspond to the early days after Jackson's victory at New Orleans. As Americans developed a new sense of their self-reliance and independence from Europe, they came to a full awareness of the vast unspoiled area of land which lay west of the eastern mountain chain. Once again it is the "virgin land" which had such an enormous effect on the American imagination.*

The second distinguishable phase of development is one in which the hopeful vision degenerates as the original significance of its insight is challenged, gradually fades, and is finally exhausted. On the loftiest level once again, this is the period after the image "work[ed] its way to the surface of American expression."[26] As the pristine vision of the Adamic figure emerged clear and bright, dissenting voices arose. The members of the party of Irony began to be heard counseling caution and warning of the dangers of a belief in total innocence and radical self-reliance which breeds the ancient sin of hubris and the rhythm of

---

*Unlike Smith, Lewis makes no specific reference to the influence of great empty and unknown land on the imagination of American writers. Nonetheless, the sense of the land broods in the background of the work of the writers of the period that Lewis discusses. See Lewis's chapter 1: "The Case against the Past" and chapter 2: "The New Adam: Holmes and Whitman."

tragedy. Henry James, Sr., was "struck" by the vulnerability of the ideal of solitary innocence; James, that is to say, "felt in advance the destitution of the isolated private personality."[27] In Melville the voice of Irony is at its peak precisely because the other voices are fused in him. The "moral visions of the party of Hope and the party of Memory ... could be grasped and expounded only by someone who had already by an effort of will and intelligence transcended them both. By the time he wrote *Moby-Dick,* Melville had dissociated himself in scorn from what he now regarded as the moral childishness of the hopeful. But he was not blind to that hypnosis by evil which a bankrupt Calvinism had visited upon the nostalgic."[28] The decay of Hope's pristine vision of Adam is evident in many works. But the pivotal works mentioned by Lewis, *The Marble Faun, Billy Budd,* and *The Golden Bowl,* are all novels which appeared between 1860 and 1904. It is clear that as the Adamic symbol became fully articulated and as the hopeful imagery became an actual model for fiction, a process of deterioration set in such that the image began to change.

The phase of Lewis's discussion centering in the period before 1860 corresponds on the level of the physical source to the growing crisis in slavery, a crisis of both economics and conscience, resulting in a fratricidal bloodbath; after 1860 the discussion corresponds to the disappearance of the free lands of the frontier, indeed the exhaustion of that ideal virgin land, and the growing awareness of its exhaustion.* The bulletin of the Superintendent of the Census which was so important to Frederick Jackson Turner sets the date of the frontier's close at 1880,[29] almost exactly midway between *The Marble Faun* (1860) and *The Golden Bowl* (1904). Changes on the loftiest level of culture reflect changes at the physical source. What Lewis suggests is that American fiction can be understood only holistically. "For what some novelists were to discover was that the story implicit in American experience had to do with an Adamic person, springing from nowhere, outside time, at home only in the presence of nature and God, who is

---

*In *The American Adam* Lewis is concerned neither with illustrating the causal connection between the physical source and the cultural level nor with the parallels between them. But a connection nevertheless can be extrapolated from what we actually know of the historical facts of the period together with the sense of the physical source which pervades Lewis's work.

thrust by circumstances into an actual world and an actual age. American fiction grew out of the attempt to chart the impacts which ensued, both upon Adam and upon the world he is thrust into."[30]

The importance of Lewis's discussion of *The Bear* is doubled in the light of our extrapolation of the pattern of the American myth. What is the significance of the story's setting in the 1870s and 1880s in the Mississippi wilderness? Side by side with the unique "American idea" of a "radical moral freedom" in a "new unspoiled area," Lewis points out, "Faulkner locates his image in time at the very moment when the frontier was disappearing. Insofar as *The Bear* is a story about death, it is about the death of the frontier world; and to a very limited degree it may be regarded as a narrative enactment of the historic development elaborated in Turner's famous essay."[31] *The Bear* is Faulkner's look backward at the Adamic dialogue. It is the story of the end of innocence and the end of an ideal of innocence which had been supported by a physical source − the frontier world in which Americans lived. Those novels of the party of Irony, *Moby Dick, Billy Budd, The Marble Faun,* and *The Golden Bowl,* had all recognized and pointed out the dangers of innocence as did all the work of the party of Irony. *The Bear,* written in the late 1930s about the 1880s, went further.

As the story opens, Ike McCaslin reflects all the pure innocence of the pristine image of the American Adam. But Faulkner's hero, declares Lewis, examines "the myth to see where it went wrong; and he concludes, not that the new world is devoid of evil but that evil was brought into it with the first settlers." "Ike McCaslin," says Lewis, "is the first of Faulkner's characters to understand American history."[32] It is here then, in this story called pivotal by Lewis, that a new insight occurs from which perhaps a new myth and a new image may emerge. Ike McCaslin is free, "we may say, innocent; but in a crucially new sense." For the quality of innocence undergoes a profound dialectical transformation in *The Bear* and "in the moral world of *The Bear* a primary purity, fundamentally materialistic and suggested by the physical purity of the land, is transcended as a dangerous illusion; and for it there is substituted a purity and a freedom much tougher and far more durable. This innocence is an achievement, not merely a gift."[33]

This achievement is a mark of maturity; it is the achievement of conscience, something the Ironic party, even Melville, had not achieved without the intervention of tragedy. Even Billy Budd fell, as Adam fell, the victim of the inevitable tragedy of his own personification of untranscended innocence. Billy Budd is "as guileless, as trusting, as *loving*," in a word, as innocent, when he is hanged as when we discover him in the story's opening pages.[34]

The discussion has carried us somewhat beyond the bounds of *The American Adam,* yet it is obvious that Lewis's exploration of *The Bear* could easily function as a final chapter of that book or perhaps as the introductory chapter of a new book which traces the rhythms of the American myth of innocence in the decades following the 1880s. In Faulkner's vision the myth has moved into a new phase, the theme of innocence still central with a new form and with a new and mature insight.

Lewis does not trace the myth any farther. But if we project into the future on the basis of Lewis's discussion, the Adamic form, established and integrated into the cultural continuum, will persist indefinitely on the loftiest level with metamorphosed significance and altered function. On the level of human action, there will be a search for "new frontiers" so long as the image bears any semblance of its original significance. The pattern I have been describing may be illustrated quite simply, as in figure 2.

One of the things to notice besides its holistic character is the instrumental nature of the myth. The dialogue on the loftiest level is an exploration of the various possibilities of choice in the culture. These choices involve various courses of action on the level of the physical source. It is a reciprocal relation throughout. The dialogue crystallizes the self-interpretation of the culture into imaginative terms. That is, the self-interpretation is symbolized by the myth and is particularly crystallized by the controlling image of the myth: the Adamic figure of innocence. But this image is in turn instrumental in supporting the choices actually made on the level of human action. It is inextricably bound to culture on the level of the physical source. In Lewis's framework, as we shall see, there are suggestive connections with the archetypal themes of primordial mythopoesis. Yet even here the myth

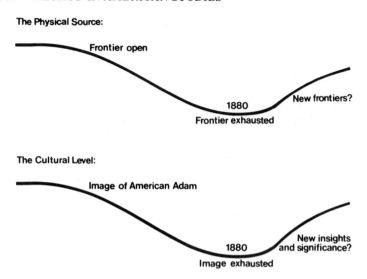

Figure 2. The cultural pattern

is determined almost entirely by the culture out of which it has grown and the particular shape of American culture at its lower levels is responsible for the particular shape of the myth. The myth is the vehicle in which cultural tensions — the opposed voices of the debate — are unified and in a sense resolved. The debate and the myth can only be understood as they relate to the dominant ideological concerns of the whole culture.

Problems and Accomplishments

The most patent problem raised by *The American Adam* provoked Sherman Paul and Kenneth S. Lynn in separate reviews to challenge Lewis on a single typical point of his method: his use of the "representative anecdote." The method presents several alternatives. Ostensibly unimportant meanings of a work are pared away or one meaning is generalized or one passage is emphasized to the exclusion of others. Any of these alternatives yields the representative anecdote of a work which is then presented as evidence for the thesis supported by the author. But Paul believes the paring process can lead, and in *The American Adam* does lead, to distortion of evidence as "in the case of *Billy Budd* where the reading provides no hint of the significance of Captain Vere and no suggestion of the anger and sense of injustice that Melville provokes."[35]

Seeking evidence to support a presupposed thesis, ignoring irrelevant and downright contradictory portions of the text, thereby rendering the thesis unassailable, is at best a dubious procedure. But Lewis combines a thesis about American character with a hypothesis of continuity. Together they tend to be radically self-fulfilling, for not only can whole portions of a text be ignored but whole texts by the same and by other authors can be ignored as well. Lynn comments: "To prove the innocence of the American hero, Mr. Lewis begins by avoiding Franklin although it is almost inconceivable that a book could be written on the American character without at least a chapter devoted to him."[36] Aside from whether Franklin's themes are ubiquitous in American thought, surely we must admit that the effectiveness of the representative anecdote is limited unless other kinds of evidence are presented along with it. The kind or even the variety of representative anecdotes which a single work will yield is limited only by the paucity of a reader's imagination.

A more telling difficulty in Lewis's method is the discrepancy between what he says he hopes to illustrate through tracing the culture dialogue and what actually comes out of his examination. First of all, it was not so much a dialogue which took place as it was a conversation in which can be distinguished "at least *three* voices (sometimes more)." These three voices of Hope, Memory, and Irony, we are told, are more or less constantly noisy, since American culture is actually the product of the "lively interplay of all three." Out of this interplay emerges the American myth with its central symbol, the American Adam. Yet as Professor Lynn is quick to point out "there is no lively interplay, no dominant clash, no dialogue in the book, for the party of Memory is unrepresented."[37] What are the names of those men who actually belonged to the party of Memory? We are never told. Beyond a longing for the past and the belief in original sin, their credo is left rather vague. How can the symbol of the American Adam respresent a synthesis of the dialogue between Hope and Memory then? It seems that the new man, the symbol of innocence and unfallen human nature, is actually, at first at least, a pure and untainted representative of the party of Hope. He may be scorned by Memory and distrusted by Irony, but he is not their creation.

Does this discredit Lewis's major thesis that there were three voices? The answer, I think, is no. Memory, we must assume, was part of the general background out of which Hope was born. Lewis at one point emphasizes that America's pulpits were filled with "the nostalgic." Theirs was the dominant legacy to the culture in the early nineteenth century.[38] It was perhaps a fading voice of Memory reflected in Irony that echoes in Lewis's discussion. Doubting its reality, as Lynn does, is, however, difficult to countenance.

In the last analysis, Lewis's most important accomplishment lies in *what* he is attempting to do completely aside from whether or not he is successful. Like John William Ward, Roy Harvey Pearce, and Henry Nash Smith, Lewis is deeply interested in human values. As Pearce clearly sees, language used imaginatively transmits, above all, values, "an awareness of the infinite degree of choice involved in being 'for' or 'against' something; of wanting or not wanting it, of desiring or fearing it, and also the means of knowing, projecting, and judging that awareness."[39] It is, after all, human values that the conversation at the loftiest level of culture is all about. All the pairs of ideas in the cultural dialogue project the immanent clash of values: good-evil, innocence-experience, novelty-tradition, and so on. Values presuppose action, and consequently Lewis is interested in literature, theology, and history, those three areas of thought that deal chiefly with the concrete moral, ethical, and political relationships between man and man. The point at which the discussion of ideas in these three areas intersects is an image of the American Adam, the central persona of this drama of human action. But values do not exist in a vacuum. Again, as Pearce sees, they must have their proper ambience. Values like poetry have their life only *in* a world.[40] Lewis's work, equally as much as Pearce's, is surely an illustration of the extent to which values are charged with the life that emerges from a particular world as life in a world is charged with values. Lewis's main effort is to locate these values in a particular time, in a particular place, and to show that imagination, value, and man's world are inseparable.

The thrust of the joint effort of these men raises again the question of the ostensible timelessness of mythic themes. In the work of Pearce, Smith, and Ward, the methodological implications of holism (which stresses cultural insularity) seem to result in those authors' aversion to confronting the question of the continuity of mythic themes across cultures throughout history. Lewis at times is similarly reluctant. Even when he refers to the Freudian overtones of some works (the psychological novels of Oliver Wendell Holmes are an example),[41] his discussion seems more an aside than an integral portion of the text and the reader may wonder why it is included at all. The same is true of brief references to Thoreau and the Jungian themes of *Walden*.[42]

Yet Lewis also attempts to meet the problem. He sees the American myth characterized by the Christian myth of the Fall of Man. Moreover, in the key essay "The Hero in the New World: William Faulkner's *The Bear*," Lewis turns his full attention from the myth's American locus to the timeless thematic material: "Isaac's achievement is the achievement of his creator, working an astonishing alchemical change on specifically American materials: converting not only history into art, but illusion into reality and converting qualities like innocence from a lower to a higher order of value."[43] This conversion moves away from the temporal particular so that even though it is "grounded historically and built out of the moral dilemmas which the history gave rise to, *The Bear* no less impressively reflects a timeless psychic drama."[44] The recognition of this duplicity of myth, its double role and function and its dual source, is surely one of Lewis's most significant achievements.

VI

The Achievements and Limitations of Organic Holism

*Holism and the Problem
of Language*

Each of the four writers discussed in this book has made important substantive contributions to American Studies as a discipline, but more importantly they have contributed significantly to its method. Their work forms a paradigm of the holistic approach to the study of American culture. The writing of Pearce, Smith, Ward, and Lewis exhibits the intrinsic weaknesses of the method, but their accomplishments are still highly suggestive and worthy of close study. Having examined them in some detail, we are now in a position to pull together some of the loose strands of this account and consider at greater length some of the contributions and problems which have emerged. Although all four writers are committed to a holistic approach to myth and culture, each has a unique idea of the way the holistic approach might be made.

From a purely logical point of view, Pearce's theory of the poet's relationship to the deepest levels of culture through language seems to have the best constructed theoretical framework. It clearly has a wide range of applications in the study of culture and its richest significance, as a tool for the analysis of value and cultural change, will be discussed later in this chapter.

Smith's major contribution is not so much in the area of systematic theory as in the stimulus he has given to the entire study of American culture. It is worth repeating that *Virgin Land* is a pioneering effort to treat literature as a part of cultural history while at the same time recognizing that literature is more than merely documentary grist for the intellectual historian's mill.

Ward's special contribution is to show how an essentially political image managed to become a dramatic cultural symbol by projecting the major ideals of the age. By carrying Smith's work a step further, Ward demonstrates how cultural myths are engendered.

One of the most important contributions of R. W. B. Lewis is his re-creation of the conversation about American experience. Too often in the past, only two sides of the conversation have been heard. It is Lewis's merit that he has kept an ear open for another voice which also forms part of a viable tradition in America, a voice which had been less prominent because so many of its early spokesmen were minor figures. Lewis's theme in *The American Adam* is underscored by the lesson of the last few years that a cultural conversation as simple as a dialogue is no longer possible, if indeed it ever was. The cultural dialogue is really a full-scale panel discussion among a plurality of cultures, a discussion only beginning to show up in the literature and art of the nation. One problem for the future will be to characterize the other voices with respect to the conversation as described by Lewis. Do they articulate something wholly and radically new?

The major contribution of Pearce, Smith, Ward, and Lewis, however, is one which they made in common. It is also one which is understandable only after a reading of all four men reveals that their joint effort has enormous consequences for modern cultural history. Their work is an answer to one of the most critical intellectual challenges of the twentieth century.

The fruit of much modern American literary criticism has been an extreme isolationist attitude on the part of many literary scholars and the resultant removal of literary scholarship from any concern with the circumstances of man's existential condition. In terror at the historical development of American culture and the dehumanizing encroachment of a highly technological civilization, some critics passionately revived the old struggle between science and poetry. This was particularly true of those southern critics who had come to believe that America was a barbaric nation because it either lacked or rejected history. These critics saw the tradition of the South as the only viable humanizing tradition for the future. Men like John Crowe Ransom, Allen Tate, and Robert Penn Warren saw in modern science a gross and dangerous enemy. Particularly exasperating to these writers were the reductionist and relativistic tendencies of scientific and naturalistic theories of all kinds (historical, sociological, or psychological), which insisted on a thorough continuity of analysis between scientific method and all areas of human behavior including literature.

The New Critics were not the first thinkers to have felt the tension between poetry and science. The dichotomy has been incorporated into certain attitudes that can be traced all the way back to Plato. But the tradition of these writers is that which grew mainly out of the seventeenth century. It is a tradition nourished by such humorless sayings as "Descartes cut the throat of poetry." It is also a tradition which culminated in nineteenth- and twentieth-century positivism. And herein lies a paradox, for the theory of language promulgated by I. A. Richards and accepted by the New Critics was the theory of language proposed by linguistic philosophers as the very core of the positivist movement. It is important to understand this theory of language in order to contrast it with the theory of language held by the holists.

The work of I. A. Richards embraces one of the historical ironies of the modern age. Since the seventeenth century, art, while abandoning to science its classical claim to represent reality with more fidelity than any other of man's endeavors, has often turned toward the antagonist an envious eye, if not a worshipful one. The tools of science have been borrowed by the humanities and put to new uses. The methods of the sciences have been adopted as artistic and critical assumptions. Marjorie Nicholson has repeatedly demonstrated in her work the close connection between the development of science in the eighteenth century and the parallel development of the English literary imagination.[1] In itself then the psychologizing tendency in Richards's theory of language is not unusual, especially when we recall the proliferation in the twentieth century of psychological theories of art. At first glance Richards seems simply to have fallen in behind Freud and Watson. The irony appears in Richards in the fervor with which he courts science — not in desperation, but with a joyous enthusiasm. Not since Taine has there been a more radically scientistic approach to poetry. But to discover that Richards is radical in his approach to poetry is to discover that he, unlike Taine, is conservative in his aims.

The theory of language Richards adopted and helped to popularize as the study of semantics was developed by the logical positivists. The positivists raised a critical storm over their ideas of the appropriate function of language and their theory of meaning. The theory was not new; it had a venerable history. However, by rigorously elucidating the theory, clarifying the basic distinctions it contained, and suggesting the criterion of meaning they believed it involved, the positivists raised it to the level of a powerful analytic tool.

They set out to distinguish between two basic types of meaningful statements: analytic and synthetic. Analytic statements are those which can be known to be true or false merely by an examination of the meanings of the terms involved. An example is "All octogenarians are more than ten years old." To prove this, we do not need to take a census of all octogenarians; all we need to do is to understand the meanings of the terms used in the assertion. John Locke called such statements "trifling propositions," though this name is misleading, since not all of them are "trifling" in the sense of being unimportant.[2] David Hume called them propositions expressing "relations between ideas"; Immanuel Kant, "analytic propositions"; Ludwig Wittgenstein, "tautologies."[3]

Synthetic statements are those which cannot be known to be true or false by an examination of the meanings of the terms involved. Empiricists have traditionally maintained that such statements can only be validated or invalidated by reference to experience, and the positivists followed traditional empiricism in insisting upon this. An example of this type of statement is "All octogenarians have gray hair." In order to be able to validate this statement, it is not enough merely to understand the meanings of the terms used (though that is, of course, necessary); we must also observe all octogenarians.

The positivists believed that the distinction they made between analytic and synthetic statements was based on the only two ways in which statements can be verified. There was, however, a question which remained to be answered. What about the innumerable statements which cannot be verified in either of the ways in which analytic and synthetic statements are verified?

The positivists no doubt believed that the answer was obvious, for out of the analytic-synthetic distinction grew their theory of literal meaning. Perhaps the best statement of the theory of literal meaning and its repugnant consequences is made by Alfred Jules Ayer. Ayer says that he wants to set forth "the rule which determines the literal significance of language." "Our charge against the metaphysician," he writes, "is not that he attempts to employ the understanding in a field where it cannot profitably venture, but that he produces sentences which fail to conform to the conditions under which alone a sentence can be literally significant."[4] The criterion of the meaningfulness of statements which purport to be statements of fact is that

> a sentence is [meaningful] to any given person, if, and only if, he knows how to verify the proposition which it purports to express — that is, if he knows what observations would lead him, under certain conditions, to accept the proposition as being true, or reject it as being false. If, on the other hand, the putative proposition is of such a character that the assumption of its truth, or falsehood, is consistent with any assumption whatsoever concerning the nature of his future experience, then, as far as he is concerned, it is, if not a tautology, a mere pseudo-proposition.[5]

Only synthetic statements are factually significant. Analytic statements carry no factual information; their meaning lies in their expression of significant relations between symbols. By far the most important consequences of this theory are that all *meaningful* statements *must* be either analytic or synthetic and that synthetic statements (about matters of fact) cannot be verified except by examination of the facts of experience.

What are the consequences of such assertions for art? "Such aesthetic words as 'beautiful' and 'hideous' are employed ... not to make statements of fact, but simply to express certain feelings and evoke a certain response. It follows ... that there is no sense in attributing objective validity to aesthetic judgements, and no possibility of arguing about questions of value in aesthetics, but only about questions of fact."[6] The language of aesthetics communicates no information about sets of facts and consequently is not cognitive, but functions only on an emotive level. But what about poetic language itself: the language of myth, metaphor, and symbol? It follows from the positivist critique that poetry, even more clearly and certainly than aesthetics, has no cognitive status.

Under the influence of the same ideas as the positivists, I. A. Richards, collaborating with C. K. Ogden, gave the classic statement of the semantic position in the analysis of the symbolizing functions of language presented in *The Meaning of Meaning*. Ogden and Richards distinguish between two uses of language: the referential and the emotive. Language has two major functions: to designate and to express. The first is the function of the language of science, the second of poetry (and, of course, theology and ethics). Exhibiting a great deal more sensitivity to literature than did the positivists, Ogden and Richards admit that in certain cases of metaphor it is often difficult to decide which way language is being used.[7] They conclude, however, that no matter how precise metaphor may seem, the communication is nevertheless emotional and not cognitive. Thus literature reveals nothing at all about reality.

With such a view of the language of poetry and of the language of criticism as Richards has, it seems extraordinary to find him exalting poetry. Indeed, once he accepts the positivist theory of language, how does Richards manage to be a critic at all? His answer is to turn to psychology. The only way to make solidly based critical judgments is to look outside the poem to what it does — its effect. Poems produce experiences in people and Richards defines criticism as "the endeavor to discriminate between experiences and to evaluate them."[8] A poem produces a set of experiences within a reader which corresponds to life experiences in that it arouses and satisfies a set of interests in him.

In this view, man is conceived as a complex system of actions and reactions delicately poised, swinging in and out of equilibrium. What Richards means by "interests" for man is the preservation of this delicate balance. The more situations the organism meets and overcomes, the more complex and ramified its system becomes as the ability to react diversifies and heightens. This ability is the criterion for a mature human being. "It is this incredibly complex assemblage of interests to which the printed poem has to appeal."[9] Thus the source of value is in the experience produced by the poem. The real value of poetry is entirely psychological, instrumental.

Richards's impact on American criticism was immense and needs little documentation here. The New Critics' debt to Richards was acknowledged at the very beginning of John Crowe Ransom's book *The New Criticism*: "Discussion of the new criticism must start with Mr. Richards. The new criticism very nearly began with him. It might be said also that it began with him in the right way, because he attempted to found it on a more comprehensive basis than other critics did."[10]

In his work on language what Richards had effectively done was to distinguish between all forms of scientific discourse and poetic discourse. The New Critics saw the theory of language as a way of making an absolute logical distinction between the realm of science and the realm of poetry, establishing the autonomy of the literary object and avoiding any form of reductionist treatment of it. In embracing the theory of language, however, they rejected Richards's psychological analysis of poetry as a stimulus response mechanism and, more importantly, they rejected the most radical consequences of his theory: the factual meaninglessness of poetic statements. They suggested that poetic statements are not of the same nature as propositions about matters of fact. Critics have given varied descriptions of the precise nature of a poetic statement but most agree on the essential point that it is unique and cannot be understood in terms of history, psychology, sociology, or any other mode of knowledge. Nor is it an expression of personality. In "Tradition and the Individual Talent" T. S. Eliot denied that poetry is "a turning loose of emotion" or "the expression of personality." It is, in fact, "an escape from emotion," "an escape from personality." "The poet has not a personality to express, but a particular medium, which is only a medium and not a personality, in which impressions and experiences combine in peculiar and unexpected ways. Impressions and experiences which are important for the man may take no place in the poetry, and those which become important in the poetry may play quite a negligible part in the man, the personality."[11] The "medium," of course, is language and Eliot is denying that there is any *necessary* connection between a poet's experience and the language he uses in the construction of a poem. The poem has been neatly severed from the existential ambience in which it came to being.

As one might expect, it is precisely at this point, the fragmentation of human experience, that the holistic thinkers make their attack. One of the primary facets of a holistic view of man and his activities is its rejection of such an atomistic truncated vision of reality. The theory of language embraced by the New Critics was completely inadequate to describe a holistic world. Nevertheless, cultural historians who always believed literature could not be separated from its ambience were forced by the acuteness of the New Critics' analyses to spell out the grounds of their opposition.

Although holists have not individually given as much attention to the theory of language as the New Critics and their predecessors, some essential assumptions about language are made by all. Of the four writers studied in this book, Pearce has written most extensively and specifically on language, especially as it relates to the nature of poetry. In "Historicism Once More," a long essay published in 1958, Pearce pursues and develops some of his basic ideas. He is interested in the problem of history as it bears upon literature – a problem which he believes the New Critics obscured. His own brand of historical criticism Pearce calls historicism.* "The basic thesis of historicism," according to Hans Meyerhoff, "is quite simple: the subject matter of history is human life in its totality and multiplicity. It is the historian's aim to portray the bewildering, unsystematic variety of historical forms – people, nations, cultures, customs, institutions, songs, myths, and thoughts – in their unique living expressions and in the process of continuous growth and transformation."[12]

Pearce begins his essay with a gambit the importance of which it is easy to overlook. He asks two questions, the second an extension of the first. "How is literature possible?" and "How is it possible that literature should be what it is?" If we understand how it is possible, he

*Although Professor Pearce's historicism has affinities with the classical historicism of Ranke, it is deducible, I believe, from his prior holistic assumptions.

suggests, we will also understand what it is. The force of this question will be seen if we rephrase it. Since literature does exist, it is quite proper to ask *how* it is possible; for that it *is* possible is proved by the fact that it exists. At the heart of this question is the further question (the one in which he is most deeply interested): What must language and culture be like for literature to exist?

Pearce considers that the answer will perforce involve the problem of history, for a literary work carries the past into the present. It is not "just . . . a monument endowed with the sort of factuality from which we may infer its previous mode of existence," but rather it is "a somehow 'living' thing from whose particularity of form we may apprehend that existence and to a significant degree share in it."[13] In fact, one of the things he hopes to prove in the essay is that the disjunctive proposition history vs. literature is untenable: "Literature is possible precisely as it is because it is in its very nature a way, perhaps the most profound, of comprehending that dialectical opposition which characterizes our knowledge of ourselves in our history. . . . [Thus] the proposition should read: [not history vs. literature but] history (*our* history) via literature. If this is so, then we shall have again to develop a kind of criticism which is, by definition, a form of historical understanding."[14]

The formalist critics, suggests Pearce, were aware of the problem of language and history. But they have obscured the "terms and conditions" of its solution by the truncation of literature from the values of the culture from which it comes. Eliot in "Tradition and the Individual Talent" is the greatest example. He insists that for the poet all the past is totally and immediately available as part of a tradition independent of the poet's experience. "Yet," says Pearce, "the problem of history *qua* history, of what part history itself has in the meaning of poems, has always been present in Mr. Eliot's thinking about literature."[15] This is especially true when Eliot writes of the poet's deep obligation to his language. The fundamental duty of the poet, according to Eliot, is to his language rather than to his people. He must first preserve it and second extend and improve it.

Up to this point Pearce concurs with Eliot, but, he claims, Eliot simply did not go far enough. "It is," Pearce continues, "on the consideration of the poet's relation to his language that there must be centered any examination of his relation to history; for language must be for the poet the principal vehicle for history; through language history gets into literature."[16]

This is, of course, an extension of the view examined in chapter II on Pearce — poet: language: culture — with one additional emphasis. Here we see that the poem is related through the artistic medium of language to the culture and hence to the values of that culture, for language is value laden in a way which plastic substances are not. "This is, indeed," says Pearce, "of the essence of its power to symbolize. Language above all communicates values . . . and by 'values' I mean both feelings of desirability and obligation and their negatives, and the very modes and forms by which those feelings and their negatives are expressed."[17] Pearce means here much more than that language may be used to make value statements. The thrust of his argument is that the very texture of language is permeated with the values of the culture. Literature can never be "pure" or totally free of "mundanely determined value-forces" because the poet has a direct existential relation to his culture — one man, impulsive perhaps, but deeply involved, necessarily intermixed with society and nature. Our language is not a set of impersonal symbols injected into an interpersonal void; our language, being a part of our actions, is as communicative and powerful as they are. "Studying language, we study history. We study history, so that we can study language. (There are other ways to do so, of course, as there are other institutions which make for the historical continuity of culture; but this one is our major concern, because it is our artists'.) Studying history, we study culture. Studying a culture, we study its poetry. Studying its poetry, we study its language. The system is one and whole. If it is closed, that is because it encloses us."[18]

The answer to the question "What must language be like in order for literature to exist?" is that for language to exist at all it must be wholly permeated with the values of its origin. It is not pure, that is, not free of values.* When a word gets into a poem, the historical-cultural ambience is not left behind. If this is true, "to what degree is language,

*This applies even to the language of science, with the exception of the totally quantified sciences.

or culture, or history, qualitatively *in*, existentially *in*, a literary work? By virtue of being there, what does it do? Then: in what sense do we, as we read critically, actually engage ourselves to the language, the culture, the history, which is there?"[19] If, as the formalist critics agree, language is not passive but has a dynamic part in the creation of literary art, "then the effect of that work on us must be in some part the effect of language — of the specific values with which it is charged and of the form which values took, and so of the period in which those values had their existence."[20]

The result of his analysis convinces Pearce that we need to supersede formalist criticism and strive for a "critical historicism." By this Pearce does not intend to suggest that we return to the old criticism's shortsightedness about the unique and intrinsic qualities of the work by simply putting the work in its sociocultural context. In other words, he recognizes that literary art is not to be merely a vehicle for the cultural and intellectual history of some particular time. Yet we must see that because of the power of language, "history is as much *in* our literary texts as our texts are in our history." Thus as we come to know our poetry we come to know ourselves. And in coming to know ourselves we will be in position to write the "inside narrative" that Pearce speaks about in *The Continuity of American Poetry*.

Language, literature, history, and culture are inextricably interwoven in Pearce's thinking. And we may well add the concept of community to this, for without the communality of a particular language there could be no cultural community — or indeed any cultural diversity. It imperceptibly links the poet with the past. Language enables him to enter into communion with his progenitors, for values do not exist and are not born in a vacuum. They are the result of existential choices in particular historical situations. The poet, in turn, again by means of language, perpetuates and enriches the thought, values, and feelings of the past for the benefit of the future. In this way language embodies the living manifestation of historical and cultural continuity.

In holistic thinking the creative force of the language of poetry cannot be overestimated. Indeed, it is only through language that we can enter into a past historical period. But poetic language is by nature charged with feeling and value, the central elements of myth and symbol. As dreams are regressive and refer to the deep layers of human experience, so in a like manner myths are regressive and refer to the deep and rich layers of cultural experience.

If the thrust of much modern literary scholarship has been the isolation of literature from the historicocultural ambience, the thrust of holistic thinking is to locate literature squarely and necessarily in that ambience. Surely this insight is one of the major contributions of the four writers singled out here. The isolationist attitude is perhaps one of the major reasons why present-day students, demanding relevance, have become alienated from literature, ceasing to regard it as a study from which they can derive direct personal benefit or learn anything helpful to them about their past or the past of their culture. It is in the correction of this situation that the American Studies approach has been most valuable, with its articulation of the fact that literature and the language of literature do not exist in a vacuum and that they grow out of and are part of a culture which is a whole.

The interest that Pearce has in values and their ambience is shared by Smith, Ward, and Lewis. Surely this is an interest for which we must be deeply indebted. All four men see that the study of conflicting values can reveal the hidden dynamics of culture which motivate human action, and that the conflict of values is exhibited best after passing through the crucible of the human imagination and issuing into an image.

Problems: Literary Nationalism and National Character

In spite of the worth of their contribution, American Studies scholars have raised new problems which must be solved if the kind of goal which they desire is to be achieved. I want to reiterate several of the problems here as they emerged in the preceding chapters and then to consider one in some detail.

The first problem is a kind of literary nationalism that emerges. Literary nationalism may be the logical outcome of a search for what is the best expression of a *unique* national character. The search is reinforced by holistic assumptions that imply that each culture is indeed unique and has its own characteristic expression. The consequences for criticism may be insidious. As Solomon Fishman comments: "Literary nationalism ... converts the national category into an active principle of composition, a criterion of value. In this perspective the preliminary condition of literary activity is a distinctive national culture; the value of a work is not only derived from nationality but also gauged by fidelity to the national culture."[21]

Thus the Adamic mode, the myth of the garden, and participation in the Adamic conversation are at times dangerously near to becoming criteria of critical exclusion instead of hypotheses subject to demonstration. As a result, Pearce tends to mistreat Robinson, Poe, Eliot, and others; Smith neglects Hawthorne, Melville, and Thoreau; and Lewis avoids Benjamin Franklin and Melville's Captain Vere. If the writer is expected to adhere in his writing to some kind of vision of what constitutes proper national themes, forms, or style, then literature will suffer thereby. As Flannery O'Connor wrote: "Every novelist has his preoccupations, and none can see and write everything. Partial vision has to be expected, but partial vision is not dishonest vision unless it has been dictated. I don't think that we have the right to demand of our novelists that they write an *American* novel at all. A novel that could be described simply as an American novel and no more would be too limited an undertaking for a good novelist to waste his time on."[22]

Literary nationalism is not the direct consequence of organic holism, but it certainly receives an enormous impetus from a holism which tends to identify culture with national boundaries and then insists unequivocally on cultural uniqueness. This brings us to the second problem that emerges from the discussion.

Assuming that myths (as well as all other cultural forms) are spawned by the cultural whole and only by the cultural whole, holism implies a kind of insularity of particular cultures which does not entirely square with the facts of human history. If a thorough holism were true, then all aspects of myths would be unique to the culture from which they emerge. This does not account for the continuity of myths across the many cultures of human history.

The problem does not seem to me to be unsolvable, however. Certainly the specific content of myths appears to be conditioned by their cultural ambience. But the structure clearly is not. A holistic belief must be flexible enough to accommodate the notion that perhaps the structural elements of myth are somehow universal concerns of the human race conditioned by some common *human* experiences as well as by unique *cultural* experiences.

R. W. B. Lewis has come the closest to dealing with this problem. His work suggests that the content of myth has a physical source: man in a new world equals an American Adam. But since the myth is essentially an expression of values and since man faces the same choices wherever he may be, the structural aspect of myth is universal.

Both literary nationalism and the search for national myths and symbols are logically and dramatically connected with a third significant problem: national character. To look for the unique expression of the American experience, to look for *the* American myth is to look also for the defining characteristics of American character. It is to ask with Crèvecœur, "What is an American?" Crèvecœur was the first to ask the question, but it has been asked uncounted times since. The literature on the American national character is immense, and the number of answers to Crèvecœur's question seems to equal the number of times it has been asked. In a brilliant insight in *The Americanization of the Unconscious*, John Seeley suggests that perhaps the only distinctly, if not exclusively, American characteristic is "the intellectual centralization of self-analysis as a collective and personal preoccupation, the pouring into it of vast libidinal investment and the receipt in return of endless emotional gratification."[23] It is doubtful if any other country has engaged in such a frantic quest for a national identity.

Statements about American character range from the rhetorical passion of H. Rap Brown's comment that "violence is as American as cherry pie" to the most serious scholarly analyses of American cultural and national style, national myths, symbols, and forces which have causal efficacy in human affairs. This "collective preoccupation" has gone on with a high degree of intensity for almost one hundred and fifty years, beginning in earnest in the 1830s when country orators and preachers turned their attention to the question on patriotic and festive holidays.[24]

If the literature on American character is immense, so too is the literature on the general concept of national character. The concern of sociologists and other social scientists with the conceptual status of national character reflects the growing questions about its viability as a cognitive model for social analysis. At the same time, particularly among historians, its vitality and even necessity as a conceptual tool is rarely questioned. Many historians reject the concept intellectually but continue to use it in their work where it seems almost indispensable as an organizing concept. David M. Potter in his excellent discussion of the problem of national character in *People of Plenty* assumes explicitly that the historian *cannot* operate without the concept of national character.

> We must remember that when human history is broken down into a series of histories of separate nations, this manner of organizing the subject will create certain necessities in the treatment of the material. . . . Specifically, it will require the historian, as a writer, to show, as every writer must, that the unity about which he writes is a *real* unit, possessing objective existence outside his own conceptual plan, and that it is not an artificial or imaginary unit. This compulsion must control him far more basically than any patriotic impulse; for national history may or may not have a theme of glory, but it must have a theme of some kind, and it cannot have a theme at all unless its subject has unity.[25]

According to Potter, this unity requires that "the people themselves are *collectively* distinguishable" rather than merely "an undifferentiated mass of humans fortuitously located in America. . . . [H]istory must find, as a unifying factor, what is distinctive in the circumstances, the condition, and the experience of the aggregation in question." These circumstances, condition, and experience are what produce the unique traits and characteristics common to the people as a whole. "To recognize such collective traits and attitudes . . . is to embrace the concept of national character."[26] Again, Potter suggests, for national character to be a usable concept the historian must also assume that it issues from some deeper reality and is an inner force in human dispositions toward certain forms of behavior.[27]

There are two observations to make about Potter's comments on national character. First, the connection between holism and national character is obvious. He rejects the "as if" view of cultural unity and insists on an ontologically real status for the unit as a whole. Second, he rejects a simple statistical concept of national character, i.e., the concept of national character as a verifiable generalization about behavior characteristics of segments of the population at a given time. In its place he embraces a nonstatistical, nonempirical concept which posits an inner force and a core personality structure, culturally conditioned, and resulting in a predictable pattern and continuity contingent upon the behavioral dispositions of individuals within the cultural unit. The latter concept owes its origins to Freud but is most deeply indebted to the post-Freudian psychoanalytic movement (particularly Erich Fromm), which placed stress on the nonbiological, regressive aspect of both individual and cultural phenomena. The best examples of this, of course, are dreams and myths. Just as dreams refer back to the basic culturally determined personality structure of the individual, so in a like manner myths refer back to the basic historically determined character structure of the culture.

The statistical concept is rejected by Potter because in itself it is not enough to account for the pattern and continuity of themes in the culture, which, he believes, are necessary for historical study. Ostensibly only the concept of a culturally determined "core" personality implies the existence of a permanent personality structure. The question that must be asked here, however, is whether "necessity" is ground enough for assuming the truth of a concept which is unverifiable even if it is believed that such a concept is methodologically vital; is the belief itself valid?

The general problem of national character is highly complex and the numerous attempts to clarify the concepts and resolve the conceptual issues reflect the deep concern social scientists have to rescue the concept. So far their efforts have been unsuccessful. As recently as 1968 Daniel Bell in "National Character Revisited: A Proposal for Renegotiating the Concept" surveyed the history of efforts to establish the concept on intellectually acceptable grounds. Recognizing that "national character" involves not one but two highly abstract general terms, Bell elects to examine "nation" and "character" separately.

The idea of group character, according to Bell, antedates that of national character and has its origins in racial ideas. Later these became synthesized with the mystical nationalism of Herder and his nineteenth-century successors. The racial part of this synthesis, however, has been largely discredited since "for the past forty years, the entire weight of modern social science has been devoted to demolishing the idea of race as a meaningful concept in history or social relations, and to denying the idea of any intrinsic group superiority."[28] The idea of "culture" was soon substituted for that of race. World War II accomplished the shift to the idea of national character, partially by assuming that the nation is coextensive with the culture which shapes the character. As part of the war effort, a group of anthropologists and psychiatrists "tried to describe the psychological makeup of the Germans, the Japanese, and the Russians, in holistic terms, as a guide to policy." "The difficulty with so many of these studies was implicit in the enterprise itself; that is, the amorphous definitions of nation and character. Not only was there a tendency, at least in the early studies, to assume a single personality mode for the population of any given society, there was the more important ambiguity stemming from the lack of any real agreement on what constituted *personality* itself."[29] The overwhelming problem of all recent attempts to revise the concept of character is a failure of definition so that "at the most abstract and general level" they "provide statements of boundaries; they become, as the French say, *une palissard* — so many words."[30]

If "personality" has been dealt with unsuccessfully, the concept of "nation" has been neglected altogether. "Equally, there was no discussion of the *nation* as a concept: *What,* if anything, makes the nation a distinctive boundary, marking it off, the way a culture presumably does, as a particular configuration of norms, or manners, or personalities sufficiently different from that of other nations?"[31] Bell recognizes that the critical issue is that the assumption of isomorphism between a geographic unit and a psycho-social unit is unfounded. "Whether this unity [nation] ever achieves a sufficient homogeneity to provide for consistent normative or prescriptive patterns is an empirical matter,"[32] not a matter for assumption. Not only are there regional differences which vitiate claims about a distinctive national character, but class and even occupational similarities that are transnational undermine the concept further. "As quickly as one can define a 'national character' (based as has often been the case, on impressionistic description, or skewed samples), one can just as quickly find qualification (and disqualification), variation, and counter-tendencies. How then is it possible to thread one's way through such a contradictory maze?" Bell points out that even in one of the most recent sophisticated attempts to deal with the concept of character the concept of "nation" is avoided as the unit of society which is in interaction with the individual character.*[33] In spite of his modest belief that the term might be, with more work, renegotiated to establish some viable meaning for it, Bell's discussion implies that the concept of "national character" is, in its present state, vacuous.

Although Professor Bell could be correct that the social sciences may, in time, manage to render the concept meaningful, it is likely that it cannot be done without the risk of diminishing its potential for explaining human behavior and long-range cultural continuity — those very characteristics which make the concept so useful to American Studies.

What is more likely, I believe, is that the concept will be substantially revised (perhaps along with the root concept of holism) as we come to see several errors we have made. First, it is a mistake to consistently identify culture with the politico-geographical unit. It does not necessarily follow that they are coextensive (though they may be). We tend to assume that in the United States there exists a monolithic culture (a consequence of "the melting pot") within which there are numerous subcultures, e.g., black, Indian; but from the perspective of the present it is clear that the United States is a collectivity of cultures. The white Anglo-Saxon Protestant culture, having realized itself politically quite early, is dominant, but is, nevertheless, only one culture among many.

Blacks are now in full rebellion against the concept of a monolithic holistic national culture and Black Studies may provide a much-needed corrective for understanding cross-cultural continuity. Currently Black Studies programs are emphasizing three hypotheses promulgated as early as 1946 by Melville J. Herskovits: the hypothesis of cultural

*Bell is here referring to an essay by Alex Inkeles and D. J. Levinson, "National Character: The Study of Modal Personality and Sociocultural Systems," in Vol. II of the *Handbook of Social Psychology*, ed. Gardner Lindzey (Reading, Mass., 1954).

tenacity, achieved through the psychosocial mechanism of encultura-
tion; the hypothesis of cultural focus, which helps us to understand the
carryover of aboriginal modes of customs in unequal degree; and the
hypothesis of retention of aboriginal meanings of such conventions as
are carried over into the new setting, with the corollary that retentions
may manifest themselves in new forms by means of the mechanism of
reinterpretation.[34]

All three of these hypotheses suggest that a culture has a continuity
which is transnational. Of the first hypothesis Herskovits says that in
the New World the "functioning bases" of African culture were totally
removed. Economic institutions, religious institutions, political
structures, and, most important, language were completely abolished —
all those things that ostensibly condition and carry culture, including
geography and climate, were substantially changed or destroyed. Yet
the fact remains that the present-day New World descendants of
Africans have everywhere retained Africanisms, even though the degree
of purity of these Africanisms varies widely with locality, socio-
economic class, and religious affiliation.[35] The hypothesis of cultural
tenacity suggests there is more resistance to the dominant national
culture than holists have believed.

Another corrective to identifying culture with the politico-
geographical unit is the study of regional differences. American
regionalism was, in fact, the orthodox approach to the American past at
least until the early twentieth century. Some historians reacted against
the regional approach by emphasizing "the uniqueness of America as a
whole." This reaction is described by Laurence R. Veysey as part of the
rediscovery of Europe in the twentieth century. "Several recent writers,
continually placing the United States alongside the rediscovered Europe
and dwelling upon the contrasts between them, thereby have been led
to a corollary emphasis upon characteristics *common to America as a
unit,* upon the so-called 'seamlessness' of our culture."[36] Thus, for
example, in recent years we have had a rush among historians to deny
the hypothesis of "southern exceptionalism."

The study of regional differences will undoubtedly be stimulated by
the growth of interest among American Studies practitioners in local
folklore and legend, popular culture, and ethno-musicology.[37] This

should provide another needed corrective to the holistic view that American culture is an organic whole.

In addition to the error of identifying culture with the politico-geographical unit, it is also a mistake to be subtly persuaded in an unfortunate direction by the root metaphor of organism. *National character* is the kind of term that Gilbert Ryle has called a "systematically misleading expression."[38] The problem of category mistakes may be illustrated by means of cases where a man does not know how to use the concepts "university," "division," and "team spirit."[39] That is, in each case the hypothetical man mistakenly thinks that the concept (or word) stands for something which exists and can be pointed out in the same way in which the units that make it up exist and can be pointed out. After seeing Widener Library, Memorial Hall, and the Fogg Art Museum, he might mistakenly say, "But where is Harvard University?" In a like manner, it would also be a category mistake to think that the "average taxpayer" or the "national character" enjoys the same kind of relationship with individual taxpayers or citizens as the individuals do with each other. These are examples of category mistakes similar to what Alfred North Whitehead called the fallacy of misplaced concreteness.

A category is the "logical type to which a concept belongs"; it defines the set of ways in which it is legitimate to use a concept. Thus "Widener Library" and the "university" belong to two different logical types or categories and are related and described in different kinds of ways. Once we recognize this type of error we destroy the kind of metaphysical assumption which arises when we try to find, and end up inventing, a place for the kind of hybrid concept which results when we credit a concept of one logical type with the relations and descriptions appropriate to a concept belonging to another logical type. If we ask where the average taxpayer was yesterday at nine o'clock, and are puzzled, we might be tempted to invent a "place" for him, which it would not be necessary to invent at all if we had continued to discuss the average taxpayer only in terms appropriate to its own logical type. So too if we are concerned with "national character," we may be tempted to hypostatize the concept (much as Pearce did "Adamic impulse") and discuss it as though it is an ontologically real entity with causal efficacy. Again this would not have happened had we continued to discuss "national character" in proper perspective.

To avoid making a category mistake is to follow the rules of the category to which the concept in question belongs, and to mix or confuse categories as in the examples above is to violate the rules governing the particular categories. Surely one of the rules about general terms like *national character* should be "Avoid hypostatizing them." National character is a generalization about behavior. It also attributes dispositional characteristics to people (it predicts that in certain circumstances people will behave in a particular way). But behavior can change. Dispositions are not grounded in some mental substance that guarantees their perpetuity or even continuity. Being an American is the same kind of phenomenon as being a doctor.*[40]

"National character" is perhaps a useful fiction but like the nineteenth-century idea of a group spirit or a national soul it could have vicious consequences. Like literary nationalism, it is supported by holistic assumptions of a unique national experience. Clearly in the wrong hands or even in popular usage it could be erected as a kind of model for Americans to conform to, a kind of ideal social and political American type against which individuals could be judged and found either adequate or wanting. This kind of "Americanism" is characteristic of the very worst form of social and political nationalism. It is somewhat disconcerting to find, three decades after Hitler, American scholars making assumptions that support the cultural value of inner group experience and national myths. It is well to attend here to some of the ideas of Herder, one of the fathers of nineteenth-century German racism and cultural chauvinism. In the words of Hans Kohn, to Herder "each nationality was ... a living organism, a manifestation of the Divine.... A nationality lived above all in its civilization; its main instrument was its language ... the guardian of the national community and the matrix of its civilization. Thus language ... became a sacred

*This is a paraphrase and a reversal of a formulation by Murray Murphey. Essentially I agree with him that "to ask how personality and culture interact makes about as much sense as to ask how the planets interact with the solar system." In other words, culture is not an entity separable from behavior, personality, custom, and role. The important thing is how groups interact and relate.

instrument. . . . Herder maintained that 'every language has its definite national character.' "[41]

Some of the major ideas stressed by Herder are the view that history is "a force no less powerful and real than that of nature"; the notion of the uniqueness of the cultural unit; "the organic wholeness of social cultures . . . the affirmation of language as the most vital source of a people's collective consciousness."[42] By now we are familiar with these ideas as the holistic concepts held by some American scholars. This comparison is not at all to suggest that these scholars are racists. Yet is it not this idea of cultural homogeneity, easily "mongrelized" and corrupted by strange or foreign elements, that led to the tragic spectacle of black America for so many years knocking on the doors of white cultural hegemony only to be refused admittance?

VII

American Studies as a Discipline

The Crisis in American Studies

It is a commonplace among many scholars that American Studies is in a state of crisis. Criticism leveled at the present state of the American Studies movement is justified, but only in part and not on the grounds that are usually given. The first criticism is commonly that American Studies has no discernible method. If this charge is interpreted to mean that American Studies has no codifiable set of techniques and procedures of an order comparable to those of physics or psychology, then the criticism must be granted. But if this is the correct meaning of the criticism, its force is slight since it confuses the aim of American Studies with the aim of physics and psychology: to predict and ultimately to control. The goal of American Studies is prima facie different from the goals of physics and psychology and will be discussed in detail later in this chapter. If the charge is meant to suggest that there is no set of common assumptions, no theoretical foundation, and no growing body of knowledge, then the criticism is simply false as I hope this study has amply demonstrated.

The second criticism usually directed at American Studies is that it has been chiefly and overly concerned with the major components of high cultural history: literary studies and the history of ideas. These studies developed in America after World War II almost apace with the growth of American self-confidence and participation in international power politics. The search for a usable tradition in the American experience produced scholars, like Perry Miller, F. O. Matthiessen, and Richard Hofstadter, who discovered the extraordinary richness and the conflict of the American past. At the same time the growing power of the United States abroad focused the interest of European scholars on American culture. It was natural that the intellectual history and the literature of a country which had formerly been treated as England's provincial poor relation should be reexamined. The consequence of the reexamination was a new stature for American literature and thought. But, it is claimed, the attention of scholarship to high culture has been at the cost of other aspects of American society. According to this criticism, it is clear from the vantage point of the present that a moratorium on cultural history should be declared, and social, political, and economic problems should be intensively explored.*

This criticism, it would appear, is leveled at the relevance of American Studies scholarship itself to the whole of American culture. Again the charge is misdirected. In one sense it is the criticism that time and again has been made against highly theoretical studies during periods of intense social ferment and crisis such as the decade of the 1960s. Indeed, the crisis of American Studies is in many of its aspects a perfect reflection of the crisis of American culture. But to suggest that theoretical understanding of American society based on its high culture should be subservient to studies of popular culture, to history of technology, to social history, or, what is more likely, to efforts aimed at solving immediate social problems is to lose sight of the already valuable insights and tools developed by American Studies in the areas of myth analysis, symbol formation, and language and culture. An understanding of the structure of language and myth in particular is central to any undertaking in cultural analysis that we make in the future no matter which level of society or culture we are dealing with. We must understand our myths if we are to deal with our problems, and myths do not manifest themselves simply in high culture or low culture

*The most thorough indictment of this kind is the article "American Studies and the Realities of America" by Robert Sklar which appeared in the 1970 Summer Supplement of *American Quarterly*. His central demand is that American Studies concentrate on linking culture and society, i.e., study the whole culture not merely high culture.

but everywhere in the deepest structures of civilization as Ward and Smith have shown so convincingly.

The third criticism of American Studies is one which has been developed in some detail throughout the discussion in this book, the problem of organic holism itself. The concept of a national culture as an insular, hermetically sealed entity, rather like a Skinner box, combined with a pervasive empirical bias toward environmental determinism has consequences that simply do not account for some obvious facts of our national life, like, on the one hand, the existence of a plurality of cultures within our national borders and, on the other, the fact that myths and symbols are structurally transcultural.

One problem with organic holism is the powerful impetus it provides to the concept of national character. The impetus is a result partly of the organic analogy between culture and human beings implied by holism and partly of the belief that every culture has a unique style, personality, or character. (See chapter I.)

Perhaps it is time to question the usefulness of the organic metaphor in its present unexamined state. On a gross popular level it is responsible for propositions like "America is a sick society" without the least question about what significance such a statement could possibly have. At its highest level of abstraction it is what Stephen C. Pepper has called one of the "root metaphors" among "world hypotheses," i.e., hypotheses that attempt to account for all phenomena.[1]

Two questions arise here: Is the organic analogy a good analogy? (I am not going to question its short-term usefulness.) Is organic holism necessary to American Studies?

It may be useful at times to compare society to an organism but as a model the comparison is subject to dangerous misconstructions. Division of labor and cooperation, for instance, are common characteristics of both the various parts of a biological body and the various members of a society. But the biological process that results in the emergence of the organism is physiological and teleological and should not be compared to the nonteleological, nonphysiological development of a culture which is intellectual, aesthetic, and moral. The misconstruction is insidious and leads to imputing teleological goals to a nation. To say of a sapling "It was an acorn and it will be a mighty oak" is not the same as saying of one's nation "It was small and weak but it will be great and strong." One is a prediction, the other prophecy. One is based on biological laws, the other on mystical vision, too often demagogic in nature.

Again, it may be useful to compare a culture to a human being, but holists who use the organic metaphor often fail to address themselves to the necessity of distinguishing the hierarchy in the organ. A biological organism is an ordered whole. Not only is there cooperation among the various parts but there is a natural hierarchy in which each part is appropriate only to its place in the structure. Plato saw this clearly in his own conception of a holistic state in which there are natural rulers and natural slaves. This, of course, is to Americans an unacceptable consequence of the organic metaphor. American writers often prefer to leave their concept of the organism essentially undifferentiated — much more like a cabbage than a man.

More important than the organic metaphor is the status of holism itself. American Studies has gone beyond a methodological holism to an ontological holism — from the demand that the scholar be interdisciplinary and *view* his subject as a whole to a demand that the subject itself (the culture) be *in reality* a whole. The latter more comprehensive demand is, I believe, a crucial error. It supports the human tendency to hypostatize abstractions and general concepts which are actually mental conveniences, constructs, and not realities. Further, it confuses an essential distinction between a substantial whole and an accidental whole made by thinkers from St. Thomas to Cassirer. According to St. Thomas, the human body, although composite, is a coherent substance and as such represents a substantial whole.[2] An accidental whole, like a society, is not a substance at all but rather a configuration completely dependent on the constituents (men) forming it in their peculiar relationships. These men do not form anything like a physical mass but are discrete entities.

Cassirer distinguishes between discrete wholes and continuous wholes. In discrete wholes the parts come before the whole and are independent of the relation they enter into in the whole. They can be distinguished as separate and separable. The continuous whole, on the other hand, is incapable of any such separation of parts and its elements gain their "content only from relations to the totality of the system, to which they belong" and apart from which they lose all meaning.[3]

A further confusion of holism is between the principle of existential continuity and methodological continuity. "To me," says Dewey, "human affairs, associative and personal, are projections, continuations, complications of the nature which exists in the physical and pre-human world."

> There is no gulf, no two spheres of existence, no "bifurcation" ... to anyone who takes seriously the notion of thorough-going continuity. . . . The term "naturalistic" has many meanings. As it is here employed it means, on the one side, that there is no breach of continuity between operations of inquiry and biological operations and physical operations. "Continuity," on the other side, means that rational operations *grow out* of organic activities, without being identical with that from which they emerge.
>
> The primary postulate of a naturalistic theory of logic is continuity of the lower (less complex) and the higher (more complex) activities and forms. The idea of continuity is not self-explanatory. But its meaning excludes complete rupture on one side and mere repetition of identities on the other; it precludes reduction of the "higher" to the "lower" just as it precludes complete breaks and gaps. The growth and development of any living organism from seed to maturity illustrates the meaning of continuity.[4]

Dewey is here suggesting that operations of investigation reflect the operations of biology and physics and that further all three are organic. But surely this is not a priori true. Only the metaphors Dewey uses lend credence to his case. To speak of "growth" of "higher" out of "lower" and to deny "gulfs," "gaps," or "breaks" is to beg the question. To individual common sense, things are discrete. Gulfs, gaps, and breaks pervade our world. We do not perceive the organic interconnection of things. My desk, the newspaper, the coffee cup, the pretty girl walking down the hall, the band practicing on the field are all separate entities. If things are continuous, if the world is organic, this fact can only be conveyed poetically. But surely not at the level at which we formulate principles of investigation.

There are at least two correctives possible for the overemphasis in the past two decades on an insular national whole. One is to attempt to readjust research to the reality of the plural cultures of the nation and to the increasing demands of the struggling minority cultures in American life. This can be helpful but does not solve the problem of an integrated theoretical approach to the whole culture. We have the spectacle of an immense and aimless proliferation of new programs at major American universities, Black Studies, Indian Studies, programs exclusively concerned with women, and so on. As valuable as some of these may be, they do not serve the ultimate ideal goal of human studies, the understanding of man. They only further fragment a divided, floundering world.

Indeed, division seems to have already become a major goal in Black Studies. On a theoretical level Black Studies has taken over from holism the fundamental notion of a unique organic cultural experience and combined it with a form of neoracism. By the 1960s many black intellectuals were beginning to reject the notion of America as one culture into which everyone melted as into a big pot. Since blacks had always been separate anyway, the right of self-determination in important economic and social areas became the paramount goal of the black movement. But what began as a completely justifiable resistance to assimilation into the dominant white culture was soon erected into a racial idea of total cultural insularity whose sine qua non for understanding is an amorphous concept of "black experience," which has genetic and cultural overtones. This implies a kind of cultural solipsism, based on a combination of racial and environmental experience more radical than anything dreamed of by organic holism. I am not questioning the social and political utility or the justice of developing new categories for discussing black writing and art, or the need for continual militant resistance to the loss of cultural identification; rather I would question the metaphysical assumptions that deny our common nature. The vision of a racial-cultural nationalism will surely only divide men even further in an already fragmented world. What is needed now by cultural studies is a truly interdisciplinary method for a total vision of man and not further separation, not a vision of the difference between races and cultures. I believe that the thinkers studied in this book have provided some of the tools for just such a unifying vision and the concluding portions of this chapter will suggest a second corrective, a direction in which we need to go from here without sacrificing their insights.

Structure, Language, and Myth

Some of the most suggestive work in American Studies for the past two decades has rested on a particular set of holistic assumptions. Yet organic holism is misleading and even dangerous if it leads, as it can, to forms of cultural nationalism and even to racist theories of uniqueness and superiority. On the other hand, many of the procedures, assumptions, and discoveries of American Studies — the interdisciplinary ideal, language as an index to culture, the symbolizing aspect of cultural dynamics, and others — have proven invaluable heuristic devices in the structural investigation of American cultural forms and have universal significance. I have suggested that we should become conscious of the dangers of the organic metaphor and, perhaps, discard it as a conception of culture. The imperative question is whether the important insights and contributions of American Studies are so totally dependent on the special theory of culture implied by the belief in the organic nature of society that they cannot be retained.

Some notions, like the concept of national character, seem likely to be discarded. Others, like the tendency to reduce myth and symbol and by extension literature to a simple response to physical or psychological need, are a naive form of functionalism and will probably have to be reformulated. For the most part, however, the results and discoveries of American Studies are completely compatible with the method of analysis popularly called structuralism, which does not depend upon the organic metaphor. Structuralism as a movement has generated tremendous excitement in recent years as, once again, the hope for a unity of knowledge has been raised. Structuralism is at once a method and a philosophy and has been applied as an analytical tool in disciplines from mathematics to literary criticism. It has profound implications for interdisciplinary studies and injects new life into the notion of a genuine holistic analysis.

According to the Swiss psychologist Jean Piaget, structuralism is an alternative to two unacceptable extremes: atomism, which has traditionally sought reality in ever more minute irreducible particles, and ontological holism, which reversed the sequence. This kind of holism posits the irreducible whole at the beginning of analysis, conceived as a law of nature. The structuralist alternative, however, recognizes the separate elements of the structure, but denies that they exist in isolation from one another. They are not simple aggregates of atomic facts but are defined by their *structural* laws.[5]

How are we to understand cultural phenomena as structural? Claude Lévi-Strauss points out that "the term 'social structure' has nothing to do with empirical reality but with models built up after it." "Social structure cannot claim a field of its own among others in social studies. It is rather a method to be applied to any kind of social studies."[6] Structures are models based on observation and the structuralist's approach is to isolate for analysis levels of culture which are significant to him and which are amenable to representation as models. Strategic levels can be isolated for analysis only if a "family of phenomena" is carved out from other phenomena. Yet structural analysis is *not* conceived as the study of totally autonomous collections of data independent of all other phenomena. Such a mere piling up of formal analyses of families of phenomena is surely self-defeating. Indeed, the exact contrary is the intention of structuralism: the value of such studies lies precisely in the fact that the essential properties of the resulting models can be compared with and explained by the same properties of models resulting from analyses at other strategic levels. Such models are also clearly transcultural since the structural models may be compared with the models built up by analysis of other cultures widely separated in space or time but sharing similar families of phenomena. As Lévi-Strauss points out, the ultimate end of structural analysis may be said to be "to overcome traditional boundaries between different disciplines and to promote a true interdisciplinary approach."[7] It is also the effect of structuralism to overcome boundaries between cultures and to promote a true transcultural approach.

It is important to note two points here. First, the method of phenomenological description of "carved out" groups of symbols used by Ward, Pearce, Smith, and Lewis is very close to the method described by Lévi-Strauss. We may call this method the analysis of symbolic structures. Second, if, as Piaget insists, one of the key concepts of structuralism is that structures exhibit certain laws of change, the most important of which is equilibration, then the mistake which produced the organic metaphor of culture may be clarified. A living organism manifests laws of equilibration called homeostatic laws. A culture seems to exhibit similar laws. But cultural forms are not organisms. What organisms and cultural forms have in common is that they are both structures. The discovery of the tensional aspect of American culture reflected in the dialogue described by Lewis and the poetic dialectic described by Pearce and the discovery of the tendency of culture toward homeostatic equilibration may seem to suggest that a culture is like an organism. But it may simply be that all human phenomena are structured on a binary or tensional pattern. When the work of Chomsky on language and of Lévi-Strauss on myth is discussed, this possibility will be raised again; indeed I believe that many of the methods and discoveries of those writers studied in this book have strong parallels with the methods and results of structuralism.

The value of the structural approach is also shown in the way in which it resolves the controversy over the concept of culture. The extreme view of culture as an organism is equally as unsatisfactory as the view that it is purely an abstraction. According to Lévi-Strauss: "It seems that both the reality and the autonomy of the concept of culture could better be validated if culture were, from an operational point of view, treated in the same way as the geneticist and demographer do for the closely allied concept of 'isolate.' What is called a 'culture' is a fragment of humanity which, from the point of view of the research at hand and of the scale on which it is being carried out, presents in relation to the rest of humanity significant discontinuities."[8] So if we want to study the significant differences, the discontinuities, between, say, Europe and North America, we are studying two different cultures. On the other hand, if we are interested in the discontinuities between New York and Chicago, we are dealing with two different culture units treated operationally as two separate cultures. Since these discontinuities can be studied structurally, it is clear that a culture can be both real and at the same time a function of research goals.

"Accordingly, the same set of individuals may be considered to be parts of many different cultural contexts: universal, continental, national, provincial, parochial, etc., as well as familial, professional, confessional, political, etc."[9] For anything to have genuine status as a culture, discontinuities on several levels at once should be detectable. That the concept can never be valid on all levels does not destroy its significance for culture studies.

Described in this way the concept of a national culture is restored to considerable meaning. It is possible to study a national culture if such is dictated by our interests and our research aims. But this concept of national culture (as well as regional or racial) has the same epistemological status as the geneticist's concept of an "isolate." On the levels at which a cultural isolate exhibits discontinuities from other cultural isolates, it may be studied as a structural whole which exhibits a complex system of relationships among those various levels. A cultural isolate, then, exhibits two things: levels which have significant discontinuity from other cultural isolates and significant continuity among those various levels within the cultural isolate. Here again we see a parallel between structural concepts and the ideas of one of our principals. This is clearly similar to what Roy Harvey Pearce meant when he proposed to study one level of American culture ("poetic style"). American poetry, according to Pearce, displays a significant discontinuity from European poetry and articulates with other stylistic levels of American culture. Approached in this way even a national culture can be viewed as a totality whose essential features may be studied structurally without positing a culture as an empirically real entity.

There are two structuralist thinkers who, in the past few years, have generated ideas which have given direction to a whole generation of scholars. These ideas are especially provocative and significant for American Studies, although little attention has been given them by writers on American culture. The works of Noam Chomsky in linguistics and Claude Lévi-Strauss in anthropology are doubly meaningful for us because their most important work has been in the areas of language and myth respectively, two areas which have been identified over and over again in this book as central to understanding culture.

What both Chomsky and Lévi-Strauss have added to recent discussion of structuralism is a revitalized interest in innate structures of the human mind and consequently a way to bridge the isolation of cultures implied by the concept of organic holism. Both Chomsky and Lévi-Strauss have shown that analysis which focuses merely upon surface structure is hopelessly superficial. Both men concentrate on what Chomsky calls "deep structure," the essential characteristics of the human mind which construct or inform language and myth and which are for the most part disguised by surface structure.

In this discussion we are not so much interested in Chomsky's technical work in linguistics as in the specific discoveries he has made about the nature of language acquisition that imply the existence of linguistic constants substantival in all languages. Chomsky's work over the last decade has challenged the traditional empirical bias of anthropological linguistics and behavioral psychology, both of which insist that language is an acquired habit system, conditioned by one's culture, reinforced by repetition, and extended by generalization. According to this view, a child acquires the language of his own culture, which imposes an iron grip on the way he sees and interprets the world. This may be called the relativist view of language. If there are no linguistic universals, as this view insists, then a culture is indeed unique since an individual's most basic experience of the world and his way of communicating that experience (language) is culture bound. A culture is consequently a closed system. It is worthwhile to quote the classic statement of a distinguished proponent of this view. Language, says Edward Sapir,

> powerfully conditions all our thinking about social problems
> and processes. Human beings do not live in the objective world
> alone, nor alone in the world of social activity as ordinarily
> understood, but are very much at the mercy of the particular
> language which has become the medium of expression for their
> society. It is quite an illusion to imagine that one adjusts to
> reality essentially without the use of language and that language
> is merely an incidental means of solving specific problems of
> communication or reflection. The fact of the matter is that
> the "real world" is to a large extent unconsciously built up on
> the language habits of the group. No two languages are ever
> sufficiently similar to be considered as representing the same

social reality. *The worlds in which different societies live are distinct worlds, not merely the same worlds with different labels attached.*[10]

Benjamin Lee Whorf enlarged upon Sapir's suggestion and proposed that even the categories of space and time enjoyed by a group are imposed by the native language and are therefore unique to the language group, totally dissimilar from culture to culture. The similarities between the Sapir-Whorf hypothesis and the holistic view of language and culture are patently evident and require no further elaboration.

Chomsky's position is a sharp challenge to the behaviorist theory of language as well as to theories of anthropological linguistics like the one described in the quotation above. He has shown that there are serious flaws in any version of language which insists that there are no innate linguistic universals. Chomsky's position briefly put is this. The behavioristic assumption that the sole determining factor of language acquisition may be found one way or another in the child's environment is inadequate to explain some fundamental facts about language use. For instance, if we attempt to design a model along the lines described by behaviorist theories of language acquisition, the resulting model cannot account for the linguistic competence of a child. To explain even the average child's ability to use and interpret the sentences of his language requires the postulation of a model far richer than any possible model based on the traditional empirical learning theory. Indeed, argues Chomsky, it requires the postulation of an innate structure of grammatical rules, which he calls the deep structure of language. "The competence of an adult, or even a young child, is such that we must attribute to him a knowledge of language that extends far beyond anything that he has learned."[11] Several observations lead Chomsky to this conclusion. The normal use of language is "creative" in the sense that every human being uses and interprets sentences in everyday discourse which are neither familiar nor generalizations of familiar sentences learned by a stimulus-response habit pattern. "It is important to realize that in no technical sense of these words can language use be regarded as a matter of 'habit' or can language be regarded as 'a complex of dispositions to respond.'"[12]

Most of what we say is almost entirely new and not a simple repetition or generalization or even analogy of anything we have heard before. This "creative aspect of language," together with the additional facts that normal use of language is free from detectable stimuli and is ordinarily coherent and appropriate to given situations, leads Chomsky to the conclusion that the behaviorist model must be rejected. The only model genuinely capable of accounting for all the facts includes innate structures or a universal grammar, a set of rules of language acquisition. Even though the surface structures of a variety of languages are radically dissimilar as anthropological linguistics has observed, the deep structure of all languages is essentially the same "and the rules that manipulate and interpret them also seem to be drawn from a very narrow class of conceivable formal operations."[1 3]

How do Chomsky's discoveries bear upon the problems in American Studies method? If at the deepest levels of the mind linguistic universals exist, then the world is, at least in part, constructed along the lines of innate principles and the mind is not, as Benjamin Lee Whorf supposed, in the iron grip of its language environment. Indeed, language acquisition is free of detectable environmental stimuli except as a limiting factor that determines which language the child learns. It follows from Chomsky's discovery that all human beings have an innate organizing linguistic structure that is capable of generating and interpreting an indefinite number of sentences far beyond any possible experience that human beings have had in learning a language. It also follows that different human beings, and different cultures as well, share something of fundamental importance, and what they share is far more important than those differences in experience that set them apart.

At first, it might seem that Chomsky's argument for linguistic universals independent of cultural determination undercuts the holist's emphasis on the crucial relationship between language and culture. But, on the contrary, a particular language comes into being only within a particular cultural framework. It is inconceivable that a language should be learned, spoken, or written without a cultural ambience just as it is inconceivable that a cultural ambience could exist without language. Indeed, since no use of language is more creative than poetry,

Chomsky's stress on the creative aspect of language, as opposed to Sapir's stimulus-response theory of language, may go to the very heart of poetic creativity in general and account for the central place of the poet as creator in his culture. In other words, the creative aspect of language and poetic creation would seem to be closely associated.

Chomsky's "deep structure" is ultimately a universal grammar, a set of informing rules, at an unconscious level, which makes possible all language acquisition, whatever one's cultural environment. At the deepest and richest level of human reality, the structure of all language is identical regardless of temporal or spatial separations between cultures. Chomsky's work also makes it clear that such artificial distinctions between cultures as "primitive" and "advanced" distort the nature of human reality. Chomsky is interested in what unifies men and it is the same preoccupation that defines the major contribution of Claude Lévi-Strauss.

To Lévi-Strauss, myth (as well as other cultural forms) is like a language. In fact he implies that myth *is* a kind of language in the sense that it embodies a message about the essence of culture. The surface structure of various myths may differ from culture to culture, but the "deep structure," the grammar of myth, to use Chomsky's terminology, is homologous with myths in cultures separated in space and in time. Edmund Leach observes that in Lévi-Strauss's view "the universals of human culture exist only at the level of structure, never at the level of manifest fact."[14] Whatever the variation in patterns of myth, when we investigate a specific myth, we are investigating something about the universal nature of man. The permutations in myth, both trans-culturally and through time, simply result in new combinations of the identical elements like the turning of a kaleidoscope.[15] Myth at its surface structure (that is, its specific narrative line) is related to a specific culture, but its deep structure, the grammatical elements, remains constant. "The purpose of myth is to provide a logical model capable of overcoming a contradiction." A myth will appear theoretically in an infinite number of cultures, each manifestation slightly different from the others, until the intellectual impulse or contradiction has been exhausted. It is conceivable that there are an infinite number of cultures coordinated by the Adamic quest myth and related mythological elements, all connected by a similar human problem as well as by a universal means of dealing with the problem.

This universal means of resolving problems or overcoming a contradiction is deeply rooted in the nature of human thought and all cultural forms, not merely myths, exhibit the same means. In his book *Totemism,* Lévi-Strauss argues that the principle of all structures manifests a binary associative process "consisting of the union of opposites"; in other words, the very nature of human thought is dialectical. Totemism, he suggests, is "no more than a particular expression" of the binary process, the innate structuring capacity. Among the tribes he studies in *Totemism* the binary process is formalized by such "oppositions of the type sky/earth, war/peace, upstream/downstream, red/white, etc." The most generalized conception of this type is the ancient Chinese idea of Yin and Yang as principles of opposition which organize all reality into a whole. Thus male and female, day and night, summer and winter are organized as the married couple, the day, and the whole year.[16]

This binary structural pattern has wide general application in the analysis of cultural forms and Lévi-Strauss and his followers have applied it to a wide range of cultural phenomena: myth (biblical, Greek, and primitive), kinship patterns, art, music, raw, cooked, and rotten food, and even the three-color traffic signal — all with surprising and effective results. This may seem esoteric and strange, but it is well to read Lévi-Strauss himself if one needs convincing. As a reluctant follower recently pointed out, not only have the early skeptical receptions of Lévi-Strauss's structural analysis of myth been overcome, but now anthropologists can only "quibble about the details."[17]

Later I intend to develop the relationship of Lévi-Strauss's ideas to the work of Pearce, Lewis, Smith, and Ward on the underlying tensional, dialectical structures of American culture. But first it should be noted here that in Lévi-Strauss's analysis myth and other cultural structures cannot be reduced merely to a function of social need. Myth is rooted in human nature and also deeply in nature itself, and Lévi-Strauss's work demonstrates (as did Chomsky's) how men are related to other men and so finally back to man's ground of being in nature. Not only is cultural relationship a matter of ties between man and his environment as the organic-holistic hypothesis has implied; it also entails ties between man and man, culture and culture.

In two recent works on structuralism, *Lévi-Strauss* by Edmund Leach and *The Structure of Art* by Jack Burnham, the binary model has been elaborated with great effectiveness.[18] Throughout this chapter I have suggested several similarities between the results of holistic analysis and those of structuralism. When we turn to Leach and Burnham, it becomes even more strikingly evident that some of the work of Pearce, Smith, Ward, and Lewis is structural in spirit and in results even if not in intent.

In *The Raw and the Cooked* Lévi-Strauss developed a "culinary triangle" for the analysis of cooking and serving in primitive societies. According to Lévi-Strauss, no society lacks cooking techniques just as no society lacks a language. A culinary triangle may be constructed to represent the binary oppositions that reflect the natural processes represented by the types of transformation of food. Following Lévi-Strauss, Leach observes:

> Cooked food may be thought of as fresh raw food which has been transformed (elabore) by cultural means, whereas rotten food is fresh raw food which has been transformed by natural means. Thus just as certain binary linguistic constants . . . become internalized into the child's computer like processes, so also we can construct a culinary triangle to represent the binary oppositions: transformed/normal and Culture/Nature which are (by implication) internalized into the eidos of human culture everywhere.[19]

Figure 3 is the primary form of Lévi-Strauss's culinary triangle. Lévi-Strauss by elaborating the primary triangle shows that cooking methods and the patterned relationships of serving food cooked in various ways (broiled, roasted, and boiled) are structurally homologous to relationships which exist between social occasions in all tribal cultures.

Jack Burnham observes in his book that he was struck by the similarity between the primary culinary triangle and basic transformations in art. He contends that Lévi-Strauss's culinary triangle coincides with the form of "all possible permutations for making art."

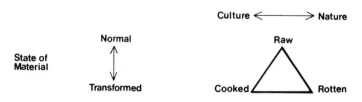

Figure 3. Lévi-Strauss's culinary triangle

He elaborates the primary triangle to demonstrate the trans-formations.[20] (See figure 4.)

Now if we recall the tensional and dialectical patterns of American culture as analyzed by Pearce and Lewis, we too must be struck by the basic similarities between them and the primary culinary triangle. We can represent this structurally as in figure 5. The binary opposition Mythic/Adamic defines the dialectical opposition Pearce describes between the essential modes of poetic expression in American culture just as the binary opposition Culture/Nature defines the dialogue between innocence and experience described by Lewis. Together the two axes define the three corners of the triangle which illustrates the structural relationship of Lewis's description of the dialogue: hope for the future, memory of the past, and the tragic voice of the present. We do not have to assume as an extension of Burnham's argument (although we may) that the triangle represents all possible permutations of modes of expression in a culture in order to recognize the significance of the triangle. It simply integrates structurally the analyses of American culture made by Pearce and Lewis.

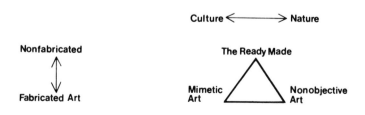

Figure 4. Burnham's model for making art

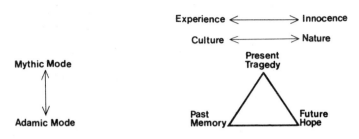

Figure 5. Model for Pearce's and Lewis's patterns

Virgin Land too exhibits similar results. The structural implications of Smith's analysis arise in connection with Frederick Jackson Turner. Smith, it will be remembered, argued that the reason for the profound impact of Turner's frontier hypothesis on a generation of historians lay not so much in its explanatory power as in the fact that the thesis itself was structured by the frontier myth. Like Northrop Frye, himself a structuralist critic, he suggests the informing power of the myth explains the theory rather than the contrary.

It is suggestive in this connection to compare the ideas of Lévi-Strauss with the last essay of Frye's *Anatomy of Criticism.* To Lévi-Strauss the most generalized pattern of binary opposition is the principle of Yin/Yang, radical contraries which nevertheless result in the coincidence of opposites. Frye argues that the informing structural principle of all human thought is of the pattern A is B. For example, in the physical sciences, mathematics seems to be the informing structural principle and the equation is the paradigm unit of the principle. The equality sign is the symbol of the identiy of two wholly discrete mathematical entities. But notice the similarity in form between the units of mathematics and those of literature: metaphors, which also assert that two discrete entities are identical. It is clearly possible, Frye argues, that the human studies (law, history, philosophy, theology, and so on) are structured by the verbal unit, metaphor, just as the natural sciences are structured by the mathematical unit. The verbal patterns are the structural units of myth and of literature and finally are the constructive elements of "the argument," for example, for the human studies and for social sciences.[21] Now clearly this relationship described by Frye is the binary union of unlike things. Furthermore the opposites, equation/metaphor, are related specifically by their homologous structures A is B/A is B. Consequently it seems that discoveries in the natural and the social sciences are informed (at least structurally) by what is evidently a universal principle of all thought. It is not necessary to agree with all of Frye's comments to recognize the curious resemblance among his abstract argument, Lévi-Strauss's theories of cultural forms, Smith's study of the frontier myth of the garden, and the analyses of American cultural patterns by Pearce and Lewis.

Moreover, Ward's study of Andrew Jackson shares some fundamental concepts with structuralist theory. First, there is the general structural aspect of the Marxist model. It is true that Ward's assumptions transform it into an organic model of myth formation based on need. On the other hand, there is no particular reason for the transformation of the structural model apart from Ward's organic bias and an analysis directed toward the search for a uniquely derived American symbol. Second, both organic holism and structuralism share the concept of homeostasis or equilibration, an idea that permeates Ward's discussion of the symbol Jackson. Jean Piaget in his recent book *Structuralism* suggests that the concept of equilibration is one of the central ideas in all structuralist thought from mathematics through biology. Equilibration involves the ideas of self-regulation and potential transformation of a structure. Thus the law of equilibration accounts for the continuity of structures without resorting to the concept of an archetype.[22] Whether we accept with Frye or reject with Piaget an archetypal theory of structure, it is nevertheless evident that equilibration and continuity are important parts of both holistic and structuralist analyses. The holists attribute equilibration to function and need but at the expense of assuming a vitalistic, often teleological, organic explanation of cultural forms and cultural continuity. It seems, however, that they are close to a recognition of the binary tensional pattern of all human phenomena. It seems also that the guiding vision of the holistic writers considered here places them among the recent pioneers, in spirit and results, of structuralist theory, which has only recently begun to attract widespread attention. We should remember that most of the major work of Chomsky was published after 1960, as was much of that of Lévi-Strauss. The organic holism of the writers considered here is modified and softened by the underlying structuralist spirit. This softening is due, at least in part, to their deep knowledge of literature and myth which has an "interior history of its own which always modifies the relationship between particular works and the culture in general."[2][3] In other words, there is a shape of things that is undebatable and radically independent of cultural context or historical event, a universal principle of structure that informs all style, whether cultural or individual.

The Unity of Method and the Unity of Man

One of the dangers of opposing structuralism to organic holism is the tendency of structuralism to ignore the historical dimension, the existential event. A number of writers have commented on this, including Lévi-Strauss in *The Scope of Anthropology* and in the brilliant last chapter of *The Savage Mind*, in which he attacks Sartre's historicism. Lévi-Strauss has several times denied any essential opposition between structuralism and history.* Yet several commentators have pointed out that structural analysis concentrates on synchronic structures to the exclusion of diachronic structures, that it focuses upon relations across one moment of time rather than through time, and that the synchronic structure is subject only to its own permutative laws of transformation and not to historical impact.

There is an important point here. An extreme form of structuralism which in fact ignores history is in effect a radical reversal of organic holism which ignores the transcultural aspects of forms. To ignore history simply raises a whole new set of problems.

Structural analysis alone must become equally as sterile as does functional-causal analysis alone. But structural analysis and causal analysis are not mutually exclusive even in the natural sciences. The choice between them at any one time is primarily a question of research

---

*In *The Scope of Anthropology*, Lévi-Strauss identifies functionalism (which he calls impoverished sociology) specifically with ignorance of history over "which one strains to spread a tenuous network of functional relationships," forgetting men in the process (p. 23).

aims. Indeed, as Cassirer points out in *The Logic of the Humanities*, both types of analysis have their rightful place and complement each other in the quest for knowledge. In the study of culture, Cassirer observes, there are three types of analysis that stand out as distinct from one another: "analysis as achievement," in other words, hermeneutic, "analysis of form," in other words, structural analysis, and "analysis as process," in other words, holistic or functional analysis.[24] Each has a different aim and each answers a different question — why, what, and how respectively. If we are to avoid quarrels over boundaries and adequacy we must see that each complements the other and each is necessary. But the analysis of structure and meaning is necessary before we can even begin to understand causal process or function.

If we insist on binding myth totally to a specific cultural context as holistic assumptions would have us do, there is no alternative but to reduce myth to some set of historical events and this is, of course, patently invalid. But what I have been claiming for Smith, Pearce, Ward, and Lewis is that they have taken a long step in achieving the goal of integrating these three types of analysis: meaning, structure, and process. As Leo Marx recently pointed out, much of the most interesting and successful work in American Studies has concentrated on the point of intersection between "individual products of mind," "the collective consciousness," and "existential reality."[25] What else are these three categories but structure, meaning, and process respectively? At the point of intersection between structure, meaning, and process we begin to answer the three questions what, why, how.* As we answer all three and come to know our objects, we begin to know ourselves "whole" as it were — to know our world not only as we have constituted it but as we are dissolved into it. In this way man will come to know himself not as an individual self or merely as part of a culture opposed to others but as a part of the deepest unchanging structure of nature itself. And paradoxically this will be the most humanizing experience of all.

*Indeed in his interesting and useful study *The Machine in the Garden* (New York, 1964) Professor Marx has attempted to study the literary form of the pastoral (which he recognizes as having an interior development of its own), its change in the context of American culture, and its meaning for American life and politics.

Fifteen years have passed since Henry Nash Smith asked "Can 'American Studies' Develop a Method?" I believe the answer to this question is yes. Indeed, the method of symbol and myth analysis is more than merely the rudiments of an American Studies method. It is the only method so far that has offered any hope for achieving the goal of interdisciplinary studies: the integration of structure, achievement, and function. It is the only method that implicitly asks the three questions what, why, how. Surely the urge toward interdisciplinary studies springs not merely from a desire to solve old problems in traditional areas by bringing new methods to bear from other areas, but from the critical need for a new unifying vision of the wholeness of man, the final goal of all human studies.

We began with "principled opportunism" but we must end with a method which is genuinely equal to the task. The form of such a method, in the words of Roy Harvey Pearce, should reflect the wholeness of our civilization. We cannot quarrel with this demand, but we must be more and more sensitive to the true form of all civilization and not simply our own. As a symbol radiates ever inward toward its vital unifying core as well as outward toward its diversified cultural circumference, so our method must seek the core as well as the circumference of civilization. In essence, the way to the center is also the way to the circumference as finally meaning and achievement spring from the vital center. Perhaps this is the great truth that American writers from Whitman through Eliot, Thoreau through Faulkner, explored from different angles. The American Adam is also Adam the original man in whom all men are one. Cultural holism was a response to the fragmentation of man's experience in his world but it is not merely the fragmentation of experience we must fear but also the alienation of man from his nature and thus from other men.

No method will help us predict the future of our civilization, American civilization, but it seems today that we are once again, for good or evil, reawakening to innocence, to our Adamic heritage. A society like ours whose original meaning was embodied in the Adamic quest myth was predicated upon the possibility of a radical reversal of history, an annulment of historical consciousness and the eradication of the effects of the Fall. This is our hope and our tragedy. We are now already entering a new period of self-examination. If we have any peculiar genius it is for that. At least for a time the new American mission will be internal as it was in the beginning. We know that somehow we went astray. Somehow, as Faulkner knew, we were unable to negate the past; the abyss into which we are all heading we have helped create. So the question of the future is not what is the *new* man, this American, but what can we become in the future without denying our deepest humanity, our roots, our identity in the body of mankind.

NOTES

Notes

Prologue: American Studies
and the Problem of Method

1. Leo Marx, "The American Scholar Today," *Commentary*, 32 (July 1961), 52.

2. *Ibid.*, pp. 51-52.

3. Leo Marx, "American Studies — A Defense of an Unscientific Method," *New Literary History*, 1 (October 1969), 75-90.

4. *Ibid.*, p. 76.

5. *Ibid.*, p. 77.

6. *Ibid.*, p. 86.

I. Holism and Myth in American Studies

1. Tremaine McDowell, *American Studies* (Minneapolis, 1948).

2. Henry Nash Smith, "Can 'American Studies' Develop a Method?" *American Quarterly*, 9 (Summer 1957), 197-208; the quotation here is taken from the essay as reprinted in *Studies in American Culture*, ed. Joseph J. Kwiat and Mary C. Turpie (Minneapolis, 1960), p. 15.

3. Robert E. Spiller, "American Studies, Past, Present, and Future," *Studies in American Culture*, ed. Kwiat and Turpie, p. 213. Italics mine.

4. Richard Huber, "A Theory of American Studies," *Social Education*, 13 (1954), 268.

5. Roy Harvey Pearce, "American Studies as a Discipline," *College English*, 18 (January 1957), 181.

6. *Ibid.*, p. 182.

7. Robert Redfield, "Relations of Anthropology to the Social Sciences and to the Humanities," *Anthropology Today*, ed. Sol Tax (Chicago, 1962), p. 458.

8. W. E. Coutu, *Emergent Human Nature* (New York, 1949), p. 358.

9. Lester Frank Ward, *Pure Sociology* (New York, 1903), p. 235.

10. C. J. Warden, *The Emergence of Human Culture* (New York, 1936), pp. 22-23.

11. Meyer Schapiro, "Style," *Anthropology Today*, ed. Tax, p. 278.

12. Leslie A. White, *The Science of Culture* (New York, 1949), p. 407.

153

13. Pearce, "American Studies as a Discipline," p. 185.

14. R. W. B. Lewis, *The American Adam* (Chicago, 1955), p. 28, p. 4, and p. 3.

15. Henry Nash Smith, *Virgin Land* (Cambridge, Mass., 1950), p. vii.

16. Adapted from John William Ward, *Andrew Jackson, Symbol for an Age* (New York, 1955; quotations here from Galaxy Book edition, New York, 1962), p. 208.

17. Smith, *Virgin Land*, p. 124.

18. Ward, *Andrew Jackson*, pp. 208-209.

19. Roy Harvey Pearce, *The Continuity of American Poetry* (Princeton, N.J., 1961), p. 3.

20. *Ibid.*, p. 12.

21. Smith, *Virgin Land*, p. vii.

22. Pearce, *Continuity of American Poetry*, p. 5.

23. Sigmund Freud, *Totem and Taboo*, in *The Basic Writings of Sigmund Freud*, ed. A. A. Brill (New York, 1938), pp. 915-916.

24. Ernst Cassirer, *The Philosophy of Symbolic Forms* (New Haven, 1953), I, 77-79.

25. Robert M. MacIver, *The Web of Government* (New York, 1947; quotations here from first Free Press paperback edition, New York, 1965), pp. 4-5.

26. John Dewey, *Human Nature and Conduct* (New York, 1922), p. 42.

27. Kimball Young, *Social Psychology* (3rd ed., New York, 1956), p. 199.

28. Bronislaw Malinowski, *Magic, Science and Religion* (New York, 1948; quotations here from Doubleday Anchor edition, Garden City, N.Y., 1948), p. 101.

29. White, *Science of Culture*, pp. 280-281.

30. Pearce, *Continuity of American Poetry*, p. 13.

II. The Poet as a Culture Hero

1. Harry Hoijer, "The Relation of Language to Culture," *Anthropology Today*, ed. Tax, p. 260.

2. Pearce, *Continuity of American Poetry*, p. 10.

3. *Ibid.*, p. 12.

4. *Ibid.*, pp. 12-13.

5. *Ibid.*, p. 13.

6. *Ibid.*

7. *Ibid.*, pp. 13-14.

8. *Ibid.*, p. 14.

9. *Ibid.*, pp. 15-16.

10. *Ibid.*, pp. 11-12.

11. *Ibid.*, p. 5.

12. *Ibid.*, p. 62.

13. *Ibid.*, p. 61.

14. *Ibid.*, p. 61, quoting Stephen Gilman, "The Imperfect Tense in the *Poema del Cid*," *Comparative Literature*, 8 (1956), 305.

15. Pearce, *Continuity of American Poetry*, p. 62.

16. Joseph Campbell, *The Hero with a Thousand Faces* (New York, 1949; quotations here from Meridian edition, Cleveland, 1956), p. 388.

17. Pearce, *Continuity of American Poetry*, p. 70, quoting K. W. Cameron's transcription of the manuscript version of Jones Very's Bowdoin Prize essay, *Emerson Society Quarterly*, No. 12 (1958), pp. 25-32.

18. Pearce, *Continuity of American Poetry*, p. 61.

19. Walt Whitman, "Song of Myself," *Complete Poetry and Selected Prose by Walt Whitman*, ed. James E. Miller, Jr. (Boston, 1959), p. 25.

20. Pearce, *Continuity of American Poetry*, p.5.

21. Roy Harvey Pearce, "The Poet as Person," *Yale Review*, 41 (March 1952), 421-440; the quotation here is from the essay as reprinted in *Interpretations of American Literature*, ed. Charles Feidelson, Jr., and Paul Brodtkorb, Jr. (New York, 1959), p. 370.

22. *Ibid.*

23. Pearce, *Continuity of American Poetry*, pp. 18-19.

24. Allen Tate, "Emily Dickinson," *Emily Dickinson*, ed. Richard B. Sewall (Englewood Cliffs, N.J., 1963), p. 17.

25. Pearce, *Continuity of American Poetry*, p. 41.

26. *Ibid.*, p. 155.

27. *Ibid.*, p. 157.

28. *Ibid.*, p. 170.

29. *Ibid.*, p. 253.

30. *Ibid.*, p. 258.

31. *Ibid.*, p. 286.

32. *Ibid.*

33. Pearce, "American Studies as a Discipline," p. 181.

34. Mircea Eliade, *The Sacred and the Profane* (Torchbook ed., New York, 1961), pp. 28-32.

35. *Ibid.*, pp. 42-45.

36. *Ibid.*, p. 13.

37. *Ibid.*, pp. 22-23.

38. Pearce, *Continuity of American Poetry*, p. 62.

39. *Ibid.*, p. 61.

40. *Ibid.*, p. 165.

41. *Ibid.*, p. 73.

42. *Ibid.*, p. 74.

43. *Ibid.*, p. 83.

44. Eliade, *Sacred and the Profane*, p. 45.

45. Pearce, *Continuity of American Poetry*, p. 5.

46. *Ibid.*, p. 13.

47. *Ibid.*, p. 187.

48. Max Weber, "Objectivity in Social Sciences," *Readings in Philosophy of Science*, ed. Philip P. Wiener (New York, 1953), p. 339.

49. Pearce, *Continuity of American Poetry*, p. 258.

III. America's Cultural Home

1. Smith, *Virgin Land*, p. vii.

2. Smith, "Can 'American Studies' Develop a Method?" p. 3.

3. *Ibid.*, p. 14.

4. *Ibid.*, p. 9.

5. *Ibid.*, p. 10.

6. *Ibid.*, p. 11.

7. *Ibid.*, p. 6.

8. *Ibid.*, p. 7.

9. Smith, *Virgin Land*, p. vii.

10. *Ibid.*, pp. 53-54.

11. *Ibid.*, p. 4.
12. *Ibid.*, p. 6.
13. *Ibid.*, p. 11.
14. *Ibid.*, p. 3.
15. *Ibid.*, p. 123.
16. *Ibid.*, p. 124.
17. *Ibid.*, p. vii.
18. *Ibid.*, p. 124.
19. *Ibid.*, pp. 125-126.
20. *Ibid.*, pp. 174-175.
21. *Ibid.*, p. 179.
22. *Ibid.*, p. 185.
23. *Ibid.*, p. 195.
24. *Ibid.*, p. 199.
25. *Ibid.*, p. 200.
26. *Ibid.*, p. 3.
27. *Ibid.*, p. 4.
28. *Ibid.*, p. 3.
29. *Ibid.*, p. 253.
30. Northrop Frye, *Anatomy of Criticism* (Princeton, N.J., 1957), p. 352.
31. Smith, "Can 'American Studies' Develop a Method?" p. 11.
32. *Ibid.*
33. Quoted by Smith, *Virgin Land*, p. 8.
34. *Ibid.*, pp. 122-132 *et passim.*

IV. The Warrior-Politician as Cultural Hero

1. Ward, *Andrew Jackson*, p. vii.
2. *Ibid.*, p. 207.
3. *Ibid.*, p. 208.
4. *Ibid.*
5. *Ibid.*, p. 209.
6. *Ibid.*, p. 10.
7. Karl Marx and Frederick Engels, "Preface to a Contribution to the Critique of Political Economy," *Selected Works* (Moscow, 1954), p. 363.
8. Ward, *Andrew Jackson*, p. 10.
9. *Ibid.*, p. 207.
10. *Ibid.*, p. 208.
11. Smith, *Virgin Land*, p. vii.
12. Ward, *Andrew Jackson*, p. 173.
13. *Ibid.*, p. 9.
14. *Ibid.*, p. 14.
15. *Ibid.*, pp. 13-15.
16. Leslie A. White, *The Science of Culture* (New York, 1949), p. 33.
17. E. H. Gombrich, "The Cartoonist's Armoury," *Meditations on a Hobby Horse* (London, 1963), pp. 128-129.
18. *Ibid.*, p. 130.
19. Ward, *Andrew Jackson*, p. 32.
20. *Ibid.*, pp. 34, 35.
21. *Ibid.*, p. 39.
22. *Ibid.*, p. 29.
23. Quoted in *ibid.*, p. 28.

24. *Ibid.*, p. 30.
25. *Ibid.*, p. 31.
26. *Ibid.*, p. 41.
27. *Ibid.*, p. 77.
28. *Ibid.*, pp. 103-104.
29. *Ibid.*, p. 107.
30. Quoted in *ibid.*, pp. 114-115.
31. Gregor Sebba, "Symbol and Myth in Modern Rationalistic Societies," *Truth, Myth and Symbol*, ed. Thomas J. J. Altizer, William Beardslee, and J. Harvey Young (Englewood Cliffs, N.J., 1962), pp. 157-158.
32. Ward, *Andrew Jackson*, p. 135.
33. *Ibid.*, p. 136.
34. *Ibid.*, p. 139.
35. *Ibid.*, pp. 139-140.
36. *Ibid.*, p. 144.
37. *Ibid.*, p. 149.
38. *Ibid.*, p. 168.
39. *Ibid.*, p. 154.
40. Gertrude Jaeger and Philip Selznick, "A Normative Theory of Culture," *American Studies: Essays on Theory and Method*, ed. Robert Meredith (Columbus, Ohio, 1968), pp. 113-114.
41. Ward, *Andrew Jackson*, p. 172.
42. *Ibid.*, p. 173.
43. *Ibid.*, p. 41.
44. *Ibid.*, p. 208.
45. E. E. Evans-Pritchard, *Social Anthropology* (New York, 1964), p. 53.
46. MacIver, *The Web of Government*, p. 30.
47. Ward, *Andrew Jackson*, p. 213.
48. Ben Halpern, "Myth and Ideology in Modern Usage," *History and Theory*, 1 (1961), 134.
49. John Hicks, *The Federal Union* (Boston, 1952), pp. 352, 365, 389.
50. Ward, *Andrew Jackson*, p. 43.
51. *Ibid.*, p. 162.
52. *Ibid.*, pp. 186-188.
53. Stephen Simpson, "Political Economy and the Workers," *Social Theories of Jacksonian Democracy*, ed. Joseph L. Blau (New York, 1954), p. 146.
54. Lee Benson, *The Concept of Jacksonian Democracy* (New York, 1964), pp. 333-335.
55. Richard Hofstadter, *The American Political Tradition* (New York, 1948), pp. 53-63.
56. Andrew Jackson, "Veto Message to the Senate," *Ideology and Power in the Age of Jackson*, ed. Edwin C. Rozwenc (Garden City, N.Y., 1964), pp. 190-199.
57. Marvin Meyers, *The Jacksonian Persuasion: Politics and Belief* (New York, 1957).

V. Culture and the Dramatic Dialogue

1. Lewis, *American Adam*, p.1.
2. *Ibid.*, p. 5.
3. *Ibid.*
4. *Ibid.*, p. 6.

5. *Ibid.*, p. 7.

6. *Ibid.*, p. 9.

7. *Ibid.*, pp. 9-10.

8. *Ibid.*, p. 2.

9. Sidney Hook, *Reason, Social Myths, and Democracy* (New York, 1940), p. 256.

10. Lewis, *American Adam*, p. 2.

11. *Ibid.*, p. 1.

12. *Ibid.*, p. 4.

13. *Ibid.*, p. 6.

14. *Ibid.*, p. 3.

15. *Ibid.*

16. *Ibid.*, p. 1.

17. *Ibid.*

18. *Ibid.*, p. 4.

19. *Ibid.*

20. *Ibid.*, p. 110.

21. R. W. B. Lewis, "The Hero in the New World: William Faulkner's *The Bear*," *Kenyon Review*, 13 (Autumn 1951), 641-660; the quotation here is from the essay as reprinted in *Interpretations of American Literature*, ed. Charles Feidelson, Jr., and Paul Brodtkorb, Jr. (New York, 1959), p. 342.

22. *Ibid.*, p. 343.

23. *Ibid.*

24. Lewis, *American Adam*, p. 6.

25. *Ibid.*, p. 28.

26. *Ibid.*, p. 6.

27. *Ibid.*, p. 56.

28. *Ibid.*, pp. 132-133.

29. Frederick Jackson Turner, "The Significance of the Frontier in American History," *The Turner Thesis*, ed. George Rogers Taylor (Boston, 1956), p. 1.

30. Lewis, *American Adam*, p. 89.

31. Lewis, "The Hero in the New World," p. 343.

32. *Ibid.*, p. 344.

33. *Ibid.*

34. Lewis, *American Adam*, p. 151.

35. Sherman Paul, "The American Adam," *New England Quarterly* 29 (June 1956), 257.

36. Kenneth S. Lynn, "The Party of Hope," *New Republic*, 133 (December 1955), 19.

37. *Ibid.*

38. Lewis, *American Adam*, p. 7.

39. Pearce, *Continuity of American Poetry*, pp. 11-12.

40. *Ibid.*, pp. 11-12.

41. Lewis, *American Adam*, pp. 38-40.

42. *Ibid.*, p. 26.

43. Lewis, "The Hero in the New World," p. 345.

44. *Ibid.*, p. 343.

VI. The Achievements and Limitations
of Organic Holism

1. I am speaking of Miss Nicholson's important study *Mountain Gloom and Mountain Glory* (New York, 1963).

2. John Locke, *An Essay concerning Human Understanding*, ed. A. S. Pringle-Pattison (Oxford, 1956), Book IV, chapter 8, p. 306.

3. David Hume, *Enquiries concerning the Human Understanding*, ed. L. A. Selby-Bigge (Oxford, 1951), Section IV, number 20, p. 25. Immanuel Kant, *Critique of Pure Reason*, ed. and trans. Norman Kemp Smith (New York, 1961), Introduction, Section IV, p. 48 *et passim*. Ludwig Wittgenstein, *Tractatus Logico-Philosophicus* (London, 1955), p. 97 *et passim*.

4. A. J. Ayer, *Language, Truth and Logic* (New York, 1946), p. 35.

5. *Ibid.*, p. 35.

6. *Ibid.*, p. 113.

7. C. K. Ogden and I. A. Richards, *The Meaning of Meaning* (New York, 1923), p. 124.

8. I. A. Richards, *The Principles of Literary Criticism* (New York, 1925), p. 2.

9. I. A. Richards, "Science and Poetry," *Criticism: The Foundations of Modern Literary Judgement*, ed. Mark Schorer, Josephine Miles, and Gordon McKenzie (New York, 1958), pp. 505-523.

10. John C. Ransom, *The New Criticism* (Norfolk, Conn., 1941), p. 21.

11. T. S. Eliot, "Tradition and the Individual Talent," *The Sacred Wood* (New York, 1964), p. 56.

12. Hans Meyerhoff, "History and Philosophy: An Introductory Essay," *The Philosophy of History in Our Time*, ed. Hans Meyerhoff (Garden City, N.Y., 1959), p. 10.

13. Roy Harvey Pearce, "Historicism Once More," *Kenyon Review* (Autumn 1958), p. 556.

14. *Ibid.*, p. 555.

15. *Ibid.*, p. 558.

16. *Ibid.*

17. *Ibid.*, p. 561.

18. *Ibid.*, p. 563.

19. *Ibid.*, p. 564.

20. *Ibid.*

21. Solomon Fishman, *The Disinherited of Art* (Berkeley, Calif., 1953), p. 61.

22. Flannery O'Connor, "The Teaching of Literature," *Mystery and Manners*, ed. Sally Fitzgerald and Robert Fitzgerald (New York, 1970), p. 133.

23. John Seeley, *The Americanization of the Unconscious* (New York, 1967), p. 4.

24. William R. Taylor, *Cavalier and Yankee* (Garden City, N.Y., 1961), p. xix.

25. David M. Potter, *People of Plenty* (Chicago, 1954), pp. 28-29.

26. *Ibid.*, pp. 29-30.

27. *Ibid.*, pp. 1-12.

28. Daniel Bell, "National Character Revisited: A Proposal for Renegotiating the Concept," *The Study of Personality: Interdisciplinary Appraisal*, ed. Edward Norbeck, Douglass Price-Williams, and William M. McCord (New York, 1968), p. 105.

29. *Ibid.*, p. 108.

30. *Ibid.*

31. *Ibid.*

32. *Ibid.*, p. 111.

33. *Ibid.*

34. Melville J. Herskovits, *The New World Negro* (Bloomington, Ind., 1966; quotations here from the Funk and Wagnalls Minerva edition, New York, 1969), p. 13.

35. *Ibid.*, pp. 13-14.

36. Laurence R. Veysey, "Myth and Reality in Approaching American Regionalism," *American Quarterly*, 11 (Spring 1960), 31.

37. *New Voices in American Studies*, ed. Ray B. Browne, Donald M. Winkelman, and Allen Hayman (Lafayette, Ind., 1966). The entire book is of interest from the perspective of regional studies.

38. Gilbert Ryle, *The Concept of Mind* (London, 1949), p. 17.

39. *Ibid.*, p. 15 *et passim*.

40. Murray Murphey, "Culture, Character, and Personality," *American Character and Culture*, ed. John A. Hague (De Land, Fla., 1964), p. 61.

41. Hans Kohn, *The Idea of Nationalism* (New York, 1944), p. 432.

42. F. M. Barnard, ed., *Herder on Social and Political Culture* (Cambridge, 1969), p. 53.

VII. American Studies as a Discipline

1. Stephen C. Pepper, *World Hypotheses* (Berkeley, Calif., 1942), p. 280 *et passim*.

2. This distinction is adduced by Barnard, "Introductory Essay," *Herder on Social and Political Culture*, ed. Barnard, pp. 30-31.

3. Ernst Cassirer, *Substance and Function* (Chicago, 1953), p. 248.

4. John Dewey, *Logic: The Theory of Inquiry* (New York, 1938), p. 23.

5. Jean Piaget, *Structuralism* (New York, 1970), pp. 7-8.

6. Claude Lévi-Strauss, "Social Structure," *Anthropology Today*, ed. Tax, p. 332.

7. *Ibid.*, p. 326.

8. *Ibid.*, p. 333.

9. *Ibid.*

10. Edward Sapir as quoted by Herbert Landar, *Language and Culture* (New York, 1966), pp. 25-26.

11. Noam Chomsky, "Recent Contributions to the Theory of Innate Ideas," *Boston Studies in the Philosophy of Science*, Vol. III (Dordrecht, Holland, 1967), p. 82.

12. *Ibid.*, p. 84.

13. *Ibid.*, p. 86.

14. Edmund Leach, *Lévi-Strauss* (London, 1970), p. 27.

15. Claude Lévi-Strauss, "The Structural Study of Myth," *Structural Anthropology* (Garden City, N.Y., 1967), pp. 226-227.

16. Claude Lévi-Strauss, *Totemism* (Boston, 1963), p. 87.

17. Edmund Leach, *The Structural Study of Myth and Totemism* (London, 1968), p. xviii.

18. Jack Burnham, *The Structure of Art* (New York, 1971).

19. Leach, *Lévi-Strauss,* p. 30.

20. Burnham, *Structure of Art*, p. 60.

21. Northrop Frye, *Anatomy of Criticism* (Princeton, N.J., 1957), pp. 350-354.

22. Piaget, *Structuralism*, p. 57.

23. Marx, "American Studies — A Defense of an Unscientific Method," p. 85.

24. Ernst Cassirer, *The Logic of the Humanities* (New Haven, 1961), pp. 168-174.

25. Marx, "American Studies — A Defense of an Unscientific Method," p. 77.

INDEX

Index

163

DATE DUE

display

JUL 6 '75